HOME OFFICE RESEARCH STUDY NO 135

Policing low-level disorder: Police use of Section 5 of the Public Order Act 1986

by David Brown and Tom Ellis

A HOME OFFICE
RESEARCH AND PLANNING UNIT
REPORT

LONDON: HMSO

© *Crown copyright 1994*
Applications for reproduction should be made to HMSO
First published 1994

ISBN 0 11 341116 2

HOME OFFICE RESEARCH STUDIES

'Home Office Research Studies' comprise reports on research undertaken in the Home Office to assist in the exercise of its administrative functions, and for the information of the judicature, the services for which the Home Secretary has responsibility (direct or indirect) and the general public.

On the last pages of this report are listed titles already published in this series, in the preceding series *Studies in the Causes of Delinquency and the Treatment of Offenders,* and in the series of *Research and Planning Unit Papers.*

HMSO

Standing order service

Placing an order with HMSO BOOKS enables a customer to receive other titles in this series automatically as published.

This saves time, trouble and expense of placing individual orders and avoids the problems of knowing when to do so.

For details please write to HMSO BOOKS (PC11B.2), Publications Centre, P.O. Box 276, London SW8 5DT and quoting reference 25.08.011.

The standing order service also enables customers to receive automatically as published all material of their choice which additionally saves extensive catalogue research. The scope and selectivity of the service has been extended by new techniques, and there are more than 3,500 classifications to choose from. A special leaflet describing the service in more detail may be obtained on request.

Foreword

Section 5 of the Public Order Act 1986 was introduced to enable the police to deal with various forms of offensive behaviour which cause alarm to members of the public. In 1990, the Home Office completed a review of the Act, which included a small-scale Research and Planning Unit study in two police forces of certain of its provisions. This pointed to extensive use of section 5 in some areas and noted that arrests were sometimes made where the police, rather than vulnerable members of the public, were the victims.

In view of these findings, it was decided to mount a more detailed study of police use of section 5 in a wider range of areas. Six forces participated in the study and nearly 900 cases involving section 5 arrests were analysed. Researchers also accompanied and interviewed police involved in public order duties. The results of the research, which are contained in this report, have important implications for the way in which the police deal with rowdy and alarming behaviour that causes distress to members of the public.

Readers should be forewarned that some of the case studies included in the report contain offensive language. The words used are drawn from police case summaries. It was felt that to paraphrase or cut out the words which were a key element of section 5 offences would rob the case studies of much of their impact. In particular, the reader would fail to appreciate fully the kind of abuse which is directed not only at members of the public but also at the police in the course of their everyday duties.

ROGER TARLING
Head of the Research and Planning Unit

August 1994

Acknowledgements

We are grateful to the many police officers in the forces we visited for facilitating our access to records, agreeing to take part in interviews, and putting up with our presence when we accompanied them on patrol. Our particular thanks go to those who undertook so much of the data collection: Tamsen Courtenay, Sharon Jowitt, Anne Dunlop and Karen Larcombe. This proved to be a much more difficult and time-consuming exercise than first envisaged, and was often performed in less than ideal working conditions.

DAVID BROWN
TOM ELLIS

Contents

	Page
Foreword	iii
Acknowledgements	iv
Summary	vii

Chapter 1 Introduction   1
    The problem of "low-level" disorder   1
    Section 5 of the Public Order Act 1986   2
    Background to the present study   2
    The present study   3
    Structure of this report   4

Chapter 2 Statistics on the use of section 5   5
    Proceedings and cautions for public order offences   5
    Arrests for section 5 offences   7

Chapter 3 Classification of offensive conduct   9
    Key elements of section 5 offences   9
    Variations in the use of section 5   17

Chapter 4 The circumstances of offences   23
    Location   23
    Timing   24
    The presence of alcohol   25
    The offenders   26
    Race   28

Chapter 5 Victims of offensive conduct   35
    The public as victims   36
    The police as victims   38
    Police tolerance of abuse   42

Chapter 6 Proceedings and their outcome   45
    The decision to proceed   45
    Court proceedings   47

Chapter 7 Conclusions   49
    Is section 5 being used appropriately?   49

References   53

Summary

Following a Government review of public order law, the Public Order Act 1986 introduced a structured series of offences to deal with disorder at all levels. At the lower end of the range, section 5 covers various forms of offensive conduct likely to cause harassment, alarm or distress to vulnerable members of society.

A Home Office review of the Public Order Act, conducted after the Act had been in effect for some while, pointed to the frequency with which the police used the section 5 provision. An associated study by the Home Office Research and Planning Unit (Newburn et al, 1990) raised certain concerns: there was evidence that the section was sometimes used where the police rather than vulnerable members of the public were the victims; and its use in a wide variety of situations prompted concern that the provision might fall into disrepute in the way that the former 'sus' laws had done by their disproportionate use against ethnic minorities. The present study was undertaken in the light of these concerns and examined the operation of section 5 in a wider range of police areas than had been possible in the earlier research.

The main findings are:

*   Generally, extensive and increasing use is made by the police of the section 5 offence; other methods of dealing with offensive conduct - particularly arrests for drunk and disorderly behaviour - show a decline in use. However, there is considerable variation between forces in the choice of provisions used to deal with low-level disorder.

*   Section 5 offences were most often characterised by abusive and threatening behaviour, the majority of which was directed at the police, or police and members of the public jointly. Significant minorities of incidents involved violence - again often directed at the police - or generally disorderly behaviour with no apparent focus. Section 5 was also sometimes used to deal with disorder associated with licensed premises and football grounds, and with domestic disputes and indecency.

*   The principal variations between police areas in the use of section 5 concerned the level of use where the police were the targets of offensive conduct or where violence was involved, and the relationship with other public order provisions.

*   Incidents tended to occur particularly frequently at specific locations and times of day, with arrests predominantly being made in the late evening and early morning at the weekend in city centres.

* In nearly half of incidents alcohol was known to have been implicated. Nearly two-thirds of suspects were aged 24 or under, 40 per cent were unemployed and two-thirds had prior criminal records.

* There was some evidence that Afro-Caribbeans were over-represented among those arrested and proceeded against for section 5 offences, although further work is required to explore this issue further. Incidents leading to the arrest of Afro-Caribbeans involved abuse or threats directed at the police far more frequently than was the case for white suspects. The greater likelihood that Afro-Caribbeans will be stopped by the police and the greater potential for friction in police encounters with black people may account for differences between Afro-Carribean and other suspects.

* In more than a tenth of cases, the police were the sole victims of offensive behaviour. Police officers interviewed supported the use of section 5 to deal with such incidents. In some cases, the abuse or violence directed at the police was relatively serious. More often, it was for consideration whether the misbehaviour would have caused a police officer alarm or distress; arrests may have been made to secure respect for the police.

* Proceedings against section 5 suspects were usually begun by arrest and charge; only a small minority of suspects were summoned or cautioned. Few of those arrested were released without charge, probably because the evidence of the arresting officer was generally accepted by custody officers.

* Nearly 20 per cent of cases proceeded with ended in bind-overs without finding of guilt. The great majority of cases proceeding to a hearing resulted in a finding of guilt. Three-quarters of those found guilty were fined, but a fifth were given nominal penalties.

In conclusion, the report raises questions about the extent of police intervention in incidents of low-level disorder and whether it is always appropriate to use section 5 to make arrests. First, although the behaviour leading to section 5 arrests is often genuinely offensive judged by any standard, it is for consideration whether in some cases the conduct described is serious enough to cause real offence to those members of the public present or the police themselves. Secondly, while there are obvious difficulties in reviewing police decisions after the event, there are grounds for querying whether arrest or use of section 5 was always the right course of action. If, on the one hand, the object of arrest was to instil respect for the police, it is doubtful if this was achieved. If, on the other hand, the aim was simply to remove disorderly persons from the streets, the report queries whether it was necessary to use section 5 as the mechanism.

The report suggests that the police may sometimes need to be more circumspect in becoming involved in situations which are liable to lead to challenges to their authority and where it is reasonably foreseeable that the outcome will be the arrest of those issuing the challenge. There is a danger that undiscriminating use of section 5 may bring it into disrepute. The section 5 provision will be more efficacious if it is reserved for precisely those cases for which it is intended: those in which vulnerable members of the public are genuinely likely to, or do, suffer from offensive behaviour.

1 Introduction

The problem of 'low-level' disorder

For many people, public disorder conjures up an image of riots and large-scale disturbances. Indeed, in recent years, much of the attention paid to issues of public order has been prompted by major outbreaks of disorder. The Government's most recent review of public order law was prompted by the Southall disturbances in 1979. In the period leading up to the passing of the Public Order Act 1986, which set the current legal framework, other major outbreaks of disorder in the form of the Brixton riots in 1981 and the miners' dispute of 1984-5 acted as further catalysts for legislative change.

Major disturbances are in fact relatively rare events. Much more common is disorder of a relatively minor nature, which directly touches far more people. Behaviour that might loosely be termed 'hooliganism' is a fact of life for many people who have to suffer its consequences. From time to time, particular aspects of this problem have attracted public attention. In 1988, for example, the phenomenon of 'rural' or 'non-metropolitan' disorder associated with alcohol consumption was the subject of considerable publicity (Tuck, 1989). Less well publicised, but of no less concern, have been public fears about various forms of offensive behaviour, expressed at meetings of local police consultative committees (Home Office, 1985).

While acknowledging that such behaviour is unacceptable, the problem for the Government has been one of how best to mark that disapproval. The conduct in question lies at the margins of the criminal law. There is a need for care in drawing up legislation which catches only that behaviour which is deserving of criminal sanctions if arguments about infringement of civil liberties are to be avoided.

A Government White Paper, issued in 1985, went over the ground (Home Office, ibid). It was accepted that the law as it stood was inadequate to deal with "minor acts of hooliganism". There were various statutory or common law provisions upon which the police could draw but each had drawbacks. Section 5 of the Public Order Act 1936, for example, dealt with conduct which was threatening or insulting to people in a way which was intended or likely to occasion a breach of the peace. This provision was considered to be aimed at rather more serious misbehaviour than minor acts of rowdiness which alarm or distress members of the public and the police were wary of being accused of over-reaction if they used it too readily. The offence which the White Paper proposed to replace the old section 5 and which now forms section 4 of the new Act (fear or provocation of violence), was also subject to this limitation.

The offence of being drunk and disorderly may cover the type of mischief that is alarming to the public but is only relevant where the offender can be shown to be drunk. Arrest for breach of the peace may provide some relief, but only partially because no immediate penalty may be imposed. The White Paper therefore proposed a new offence, designed to catch various forms of low-level disorder which are nonethless disturbing to members of the public. The key elements suggested were threatening, abusive, insulting or disorderly words or behaviour in a public place which causes substantial alarm, harassment or distress. With some modifications, these proposals are reflected in the offence created by section 5 of the Public Order Act 1986.

Section 5 of the Public Order Act 1986

A person is guilty of an offence under section 5(1):

"if he - (a) uses threatening, abusive or insulting words or behaviour, or disorderly behaviour ..... within the hearing or sight of a person likely to be caused harassment, alarm or distress thereby".

The section also covers "..... any writing, sign or other visible representation which is threatening, abusive or insulting ....". [1]

A number of points are of note about the offence. First, the conduct in question need not be directed at any particular victim and there is no requirement that a person should actually have experienced harassment, alarm or distress. It is sufficient for a police officer to show that there was a person present who was likely to suffer these sensations. There is no requirement for a victim to give evidence of these feelings in court. The wording of the section is designed to protect vulnerable groups who might be unwilling to appear in court to give evidence for fear of reprisals. In these respects the legislation differs from the White Paper, which proposed not only that a person should actually be offended by the conduct in question but that the degree of offence should be substantial. There were fears otherwise of objections to over-wide extension of the criminal law to conduct that did not justify sanctions. Secondly, section 5 does not preclude the possibility that a police officer may be the victim of the offensive conduct covered by the section. As Smith (1987) has noted, it may be more difficult to alarm a police officer than the vulnerable persons whom the offence was designed to protect, but there is no reason to doubt that he or she may also experience harassment and distress. This point of view was confirmed in the case of *D.P.P. v. Orum*.[2] Lastly, the offence cannot be committed where both offender and victim are within a private dwelling or dwellings.

Background to the present study

In 1989 the Home Office began a review of the 1986 Public Order Act. The review included an examination of the summary offences created by sections 4 and 5. Of particular interest was a rise of 70 per cent in prosecutions for summary public order offences since the introduction of the Act. This raised the question of whether there had been a real rise in disorder or whether the rise represented changes in police practice regarding the charges used to deal with public order offences. As part of the review, the

---

[1] For fuller accounts see Smith (1987) and Thornton (1987).
[2] Reported in Criminal Law Review (1988), pp 848-50.

INTRODUCTION

Home Office Research and Planning Unit undertook an exploratory study of the use of sections 2 to 5 of the Act.

The research suggested that the increase in prosecutions for sections 4 and 5 offences was partly explained by increased use of these provisions in preference to the offence of drunk and disorderly and arrest for common law breach of the peace and, additionally in London, to offences under the Metropolitan Police Act 1839 (Newburn *et al*, 1990; 1991). The research also suggested that there had been a net-widening effect and that some forms of low-level disorder were for the first time being drawn within the ambit of the criminal law. One by-product of the new summary offences was that the police were able more easily to intervene where they themselves were the victims of offensive conduct or where the victim was a hypothetical one. The report also pointed to differences between stations in the level and type of use of the new summary offences.

The conclusions of the report were tentative because the study was essentially exploratory and confined to just two police forces (the Metropolitan and Thames Valley). However, they raised a number of questions about the use of the summary public order offences, and particularly section 5. One issue concerned the employment of section 5 where the police themselves were the victims. This consequence had not been anticipated when the legislation was passed: section 5 was primarily designed to protect the more vulnerable members of society. Nonetheless, the research found that in around a third of incidents leading to section 5 arrests the police were the sole victims. It was of concern to establish whether this pattern was replicated in other forces.

Another issue related to the wide variety of situations in which section 5 was apparently used. The implication of the research was that section 5 was at times employed as a kind of 'catch-all' offence which was easy to use because of the relative ease of proof. It was also popular because it frequently led to the offender being put before the court rather than cautioned or released. The situations in which arrests were made ranged from ones differing little in substance from drunk and disorderly to domestic disputes and cases of indecency. At an early stage, one commentator had drawn attention to the scope for injudicious policing that the breadth of the wording of section 5 allowed (Smith, 1987). A particular fear was that the section might be brought into disrepute in the same way that the 'sus' laws had been by their disproportionate use against ethnic minorities. The range of use of section 5 and the extent to which members of ethnic minority groups featured as defendants were therefore points which were felt to deserve further consideration.

The present study

The study described in this report was undertaken with the issues raised above in mind. Its aim was to obtain information about the extent and nature of use of section 5 of the Public Order Act on a wider-ranging basis than had been possible in the earlier exploratory study. Six forces (Metropolitan, Durham, Avon and Somerset, Merseyside, Humberside, and Derbyshire) took part in the study, and data were collected from a total of eleven stations.[3] The forces were selected on the basis of statistical data about the level

---

[3] Fourteen stations in seven forces were originally included. However, practical difficulties in retrieving data meant that one force and three stations were eventually excluded from the study.

of proceedings for public order offences. They included ones with high, medium and low levels of proceedings for summary offences. The stations fell into two categories: **city centre**, where the public order problem was typically one of late evening and weekend disorder, closely associated with alcohol consumption; and **inner-city**, where there was a more varied range of public order problems.

Three types of data were collected. **Documentary** data about incidents leading to section 5 arrests during 1990 were extracted from case files. The information collected included: time and place of incident; number of persons involved; details of victims and offenders; whether alcohol was implicated; the nature of the incident; and details of court proceedings or other outcomes. In addition, outline data about all public order arrests during three months of 1990 (March, July and November) were collected from custody records. The aim was to obtain a wider picture of the extent of disorder in each area, as well as to identify cases in which those arrested were released without any further action.

Interviews were conducted with a range of officers at each station. They were asked about the circumstances in which they would make section 5 arrests, about the factors which governed their arrest decisions, and how section 5 cases were distinguishable from other public order offences.

Observation of policing in each area was carried out during peak times at which disorder could be expected to occur. Researchers accompanied patrol officers and incident vans for a minimum of one Friday and one Saturday night shift at each station. The aim was to acquire a first-hand appreciation of the nature of the different public order problems confronting the police.

Structure of this report

The next chapter presents data about the extent of use of section 5, both nationally and in the research forces. Chapter 3 classifies the kinds of situation in which section 5 arrests were made and in Chapter 4 details are provided about the context of section 5 arrests, the offenders (including some data on ethnicity) and the victims. Chapter 5 looks in more detail at the issue of police as victims in section 5 cases. Proceedings for section 5 offences are considered in Chapter 6. A concluding chapter draws out the implications of the findings.

2 Statistics on the use of Section 5

This chapter provides some information about the extent to which section 5 of the Public Order Act is used by the police, both nationally and in the research areas. Obtaining such information is subject to a number of difficulties. One is that data about the number of arrests made for section 5 offences are not routinely collected. Another is that such offences are not notifiable and there is no obligation on police forces to forward totals of recorded offences to the Home Office. However, data are collected centrally about proceedings and cautions for section 5 offences, and some information about arrests was specially collected for the present study.

Proceedings and cautions for public order offences

National data

Statistics of the number of persons proceeded against or cautioned are collected by Home Office Statistical Department. These figures somewhat underestimate the extent to which section 5 is used, since a proportion of those arrested are not proceeded against or cautioned. However, the present study suggests that only a relatively small number of those arrested under this section are not in fact proceeded against or cautioned - probably around 5 per cent - and the proceedings and cautions data therefore give a reasonably reliable indication of the extent to which section 5 is used.

Table 2.1 provides information about the number of persons proceeded against or cautioned for section 5 offences in recent years. By way of comparison, figures for offences under section 4 of the Public Order Act and section 91 of the Criminal Justice Act 1967 (drunk and disorderly) are also given. These offences cover behaviour that is often very similar in kind to that dealt with under section 5, and their inclusion provides a useful indication of the relative popularity of the section 5 offence.

The Table shows that section 5 is used to a considerable extent in comparison with the other two offences. It is perhaps unsurprising that it should be used more than section 4 because the latter provision was aimed at more serious misconduct (fear or provocation of violence), which might also be expected to be less common.

The relationship between use of section 5 and drunk and disorderly is perhaps of more interest. While there has been a rise in the number of persons dealt with for section 5 offences, there has been a corresponding decline in the figures for drunk and disorderly. This may suggest an element of substitution (an issue considered further later in this report). One reason why this may have occurred is suggested by the Table, and that is that section 5 offenders are far less often cautioned than those arrested for drunk and

HOME OFFICE RESEARCH STUDY No. 135

disorderly. Police officers may be choosing section 5 more frequently where they wish to mark conduct as more serious and put the offender before the court.

Table 2.1: Proceedings and cautions for offences under sections 4 and 5 POA and for drunk and disorderly

		1988	1989	1990
S5 POA:	Proceeded against	32,492	37,358	36,626
	Cautioned	3,373	3,958	4,836
	Total	35,865	41,316	41,462
S4 POA:	Proceeded against	21,877	22,927	21,060
	Cautioned	1,204	1,412	1,467
	Total	23,081	24,339	22,527
D&D:	Proceeded against	42,945	41,670	37,388
	Cautioned	15,170	13,769	14,044
	Total	58,115	55,439	51,432

NOTES:
1. Data supplied by Home Office Statistical Department.
2. Figures are for all police force areas in England and Wales.
3. Numbers cautioned for ss.4 and 5 offences in 1988 are estimates from aggregated data for all summary public order offences.

The research forces
The pattern described is by no means similar for all police forces. Indeed, variation in the relative use of different public order offences was a key criterion in selecting forces for inclusion in the study. In Table 2.2 details are given of proceedings for sections 4 and 5 Public Order Act offences and drunk and disorderly in the six research forces.[1] On average, just under 40 per cent of proceedings nationally for these offences are for section 5 offences. Three forces - Avon and Somerset, Derbyshire and the Metropolitan - conformed to this pattern. However, the first two also had high levels of proceedings for section 4 offences and far lower than average figures for drunk and disorderly offences. The reasons for these and other variations are discussed in more depth later in the report; for the present, it may tentatively be suggested that this pattern points to some siphoning away of drunk and disorderly offences into section 5 offences. At the same time, there may have been a greater preparedness to use section 4 where, elsewhere, a section 5 offence might have been preferred.

---

[1] Data on cautioning for public order offences were not available for each force.

STATISTICS ON THE USE OF SECTION 5

Table 2.2: Proceedings for sections 4 and 5 Public Order Act 1986 and drunk and disorderly in six police areas during 1990

Force area	S5 POA Persons proceeded against	%	D&D Persons proceeded against	%	S4 POA Persons proceeded against	%
Humberside	1445	67	271	13	425	20
Durham	960	55	391	23	384	22
Avon & Somerset	782	43	306	16	750	41
Derbyshire	439	42	172	17	431	41
Metropolitan	5800	40	5560	39	2978	21
Merseyside	1072	20	4125	75	273	5
All forces England and Wales	36,626	39	37,388	39	21,060	22

NOTE:
1. Data supplied by Home Office Statistical Department.

In two forces - Humberside and Durham - the high proportion of section 5 and low level of drunk and disorderly proceedings, with an average level of section 4 cases, suggests a straightforward preference for the section 5 offence over drunk and disorderly. In Merseyside, on the other hand, the very low level of proceedings for Public Order Act offences and overwhelming use of drunk and disorderly implies that, for whatever reason, use of the new provisions has not found favour.

It might be expected that the function of the Crown Prosecution Service (CPS) in reviewing cases (see Chapter 6) would have led to greater consistency between forces in the use of minor public order charges. However, particularly in relation to section 5 and drunk and disorderly offences, there may be a very real overlap between the kinds of behaviour which they cover. There may be limited scope to vary the charge on the basis that the evidence points squarely at one rather than the other offence.

Arrests for section 5 offences

Data on the number of arrests for section 5 and other public order offences were collected at each of the eleven stations taking part in the research. One aim in doing so was to see how section 5 slotted into the more general picture of public order policing in each area. Defining 'public order' arrests in fairly broad terms to include assault, drunkenness offences (i.e. drunk and disorderly or drunk and incapable), breach of the peace, as well as other provisions of the Public Order Act (i.e. sections 1 to 4), it was found that the relative contribution of section 5 offences varied considerably (see Table 2:3).

At Bristol Central as little as 5 per cent of public order arrests were for section 5 offences (assault was the predominant category). At the other end of the scale, around a quarter of

HOME OFFICE RESEARCH STUDY No. 135

arrests were for section 5 offences at Durham, Darlington and Huyton, and over one-third at Hull Central. Numerically, the largest user of section 5 was Vine Street in the Metropolitan, where over 100 arrests were made during a three month period. It is clear, therefore, that police in some areas are placing heavy reliance on this provision in public order situations. Elsewhere, its use is relatively neglected in favour of pre-existing legislation. Reasons underlying these variations are discussed later in the report.

Table 2.3: Public order arrests at eleven police stations

Police Station	Section 5 arrests n	%	Other PO arrests n	%
Hull Central	81	34	156	66
Huyton	16	25	48	75
Durham	38	24	122	76
Darlington	32	23	109	77
Kirkby	33	21	123	79
Derby	37	13	239	87
Vine Street	106	13	723	87
Broadbury Road	20	11	159	89
Grimsby	14	10	129	90
Hammersmith	26	7	372	93
Bristol Central	14	5	257	95
Total	417	15	2437	85

3 Classification of offensive conduct

The purpose of this chapter is to provide a broad indication of the different circumstances in which section 5 of the Public Order Act is used by the police and how this varies between areas. Information about incidents was drawn from police reports of offences. In interpreting these, several points need to be kept in mind. First, it is difficult for offence reports always to convey adequately the flavour of what occurred. The way things are said, rather than what is said, may be all important. So, too, may be the demeanour of the suspect. The circumstances - for example, whether the officer was alone, whether it was late at night, whether there was a fear that others might come to the offender's aid - may combine to make the situation more alarming than appears on paper. Secondly, the test of whether an offence has occurred is a subjective one: individual officers' assessments of the offensiveness of particular actions and their likely impact may vary considerably.

Thirdly, the accounts of events given in written reports need sometimes to be treated with a degree of caution. It is perhaps no coincidence that the type and quantity of obscene language used by suspects are often remarkably similar between cases. Police reports often quote language allegedly used at the time of the offence. However, it seems unlikely that in public order situations that are often heated and confused officers would always remember what was said accurately. Informal conversations with officers suggested that quotes were sometimes included in case summaries to satisfy Crown Prosecution Service (CPS) requirements about the seriousness of the incident. The more cynical suggested that the CPS would require a specific number of 'four letter words' and these were therefore supplied. It is not intended to suggest that accounts were fabrications. They may indeed have reflected the general flavour of the incident, but it is doubtful whether they can always be relied upon as a record of what was actually said or to gauge the precise seriousness of the offence.

Key elements of section 5 offences

Incidents were categorised according to their key features into a number of groups which are described below. Table 3.1 contains details of the number of cases falling into each group.

Abuse and threats

By far the largest proportion of section 5 offences were characterised by various forms of abuse and threats. Nearly half of all incidents were defined in this way. A notable feature was that in only a minority of these cases were abuse or threats aimed principally at members of the public (although they might well be offended too). In more than half the police alone were the targets of abuse. These statistics are an important indication of

HOME OFFICE RESEARCH STUDY No. 135

police officers' preparedness to use section 5 where they themselves are subject to abuse.[1] However, section 5 was introduced ostensibly as a means of protecting vulnerable members of the public who are alarmed by rowdy behaviour.

Table 3.1: Key elements of section 5 offences

Type of incident		No. cases	%
Abusive/threatening behaviour			
directed at	- police	251	28
	- public	110	12
	- police & public	78	9
	Sub-total	439	49
Violent behaviour			
directed at	- police	47	5
	- public	51	6
	- police & public	13	2
	Sub-total	111	13
Disorderly behaviour		114	13
Pub/food outlet disorder		68	8
Indecency		57	6
Domestic dispute		32	4
Football related		28	3
Miscellaneous		32	4
Total		**881**	**100**

Some examples are given below of the kind of behaviour which was classified under this heading, firstly where members of the public were at the receiving end.

> Durham, case 104: the first victim of this incident saw the suspect's dog foul the front of her house and remonstrated with him. He was then abusive. The victim's son (the second victim) asked him to stop swearing at his mother, which led to further abuse and threats before he walked off. Fifteen minutes later, the suspect returned to the house, banged on the door and shouted: "send him out, I'm ready for him". A further altercation followed, ending with the suspect spitting at the second victim. He then left and was arrested shortly afterwards.

Incidents in which the police were the prime targets of abuse or threats divide into those where the suspect's behaviour was not apparently sparked off by any particular event (anti-police attitudes, drunkenness or mental disorder appear to be the main explanations of such incidents) and those where there was some precipitating factor. It is striking how

---

[1] It should be noted that the classification of incidents does not reflect the total amount of police victimisation but indicates the proportion of cases in which offensive conduct directed at the police was the main distinguishing feature of the case. Chapter 5 provides a fuller account of victimisation of police officers.

frequently there appeared to be no immediate proximate cause for public hostility towards the police and how many incidents fell into the first of these categories. The two cases below illustrate, respectively, the former and latter types of situation.

> Vine Street, case 78: two WPCs were on patrol when the suspect approached them, shouting: "fucking slag", and then walked off. They followed him and when they caught up he said: "what do you fucking want? Don't fucking speak to me, I've got no respect for the police". He was warned about his language and he replied: "you lot at Vine Street are so fucking corrupt. Where's that slag [names a WPC]". He was warned again, but replied with further taunts of "fuck off slags" etc., and was arrested.

> Hammersmith, case 129: a group of up to 20 black people had gathered at the police station, protesting about arrests of black people recently made in the area. Most were cleared from the front office but a few, including the suspect, would not move. When asked to move he shouted: "fuck off, I'm not moving till we get justice". He was asked to move again, but waved his fist at the police and continued to tell them to "fuck off" and shouted "you're not fucking nicking me". He was then arrested.

Use of violence

The wording of section 5 does not contemplate that the provision should be used in cases where the conduct in question goes beyond threats, abuse or insults and is actually violent. Violent conduct may be more appropriately dealt with by other provisions of the Public Order Act (particularly section 3: affray) or by means of assault charges. However, in a sizeable minority of section 5 cases (13 per cent), violence of some degree essentially characterised the incident. Section 5 may have been used in these circumstances for several reasons. The violence may have been minor, and considered insufficient to justify assault or affray charges. Some victims may have been unprepared to press charges, either because no injury was caused or because they knew the offender. In some cases, assault charges may have been inapposite because there was no separable aggressor and victim.

In roughly a third of violence cases (32 in all), individuals were arrested for both section 5 and assault. And in a total of 11 cases, those arrested for section 5 were detained alongside other suspects arrested on assault charges in relation to the same incident.

Cases marked out by use of violence were separable into three groups. The first, amounting to just under a half of violence cases or 6 per cent of all cases, consisted of cases in which the violence was primarily between the suspect and another member of the public. The police accounts of the majority of such incidents suggest that the parties involved knew each other or were linked in some way, although often this is implicit rather than stated. Gratuitous violence between apparent strangers, as in the example given below, was less common. Section 5 appears to have been used because the victim declined to make a complaint.

> Darlington, case 8: the suspect, who was apparently drunk, was seen in the street shouting at passing women: "slags, prostitutes, whores .... you're all

tarts you women". He was warned by a police officer and he moved off. He was then seen to say something to a woman, grab her by the arm and punch her in the face. He was then arrested.

The next case illustrates police use of section 5 where aggressor and victim are indistinguishable. The police came upon what appeared to be a general mêlée. The circumstances did not allow them to go into the 'rights and wrongs' on the spot, and most of the participants were arrested under section 5. The details which later emerged did not change the police view that section 5 was the most appropriate charge.

> Bristol Central, case 301: the incident began with an argument outside a public house between the first suspect and his girlfriend, which led to him pushing her so that she fell on to the ground. Four youths, comprising the other three suspects, plus one other person, emerged from the pub, and set upon the first suspect. At this point the police came upon the scene and arrested four of the participants.

Whether there is an identifiable victim of violent behaviour or one willing to stand as a witness may be irrelevant for the purposes of substantiating section 5 charges if there are members of the public around who are likely to be alarmed or distressed. However, police accounts do not always state whether persons other than those involved in the incident were in the vicinity.

The second group of cases - over 40 per cent of violence cases or 5 per cent of all cases - were those in which violent conduct was apparently aimed at the police. Generally, violence occurred where the police intervened to enforce the law or restore order where some form of disturbance was in progress on their arrival. Section 5 may sometimes have been used, rather than assault charges, where the violence was relatively minor, as in the example below, or where damage was only caused to police property.

> Huyton, case 142: following a report of intruders in a derelict flat, the police attended and asked a number of youths who were present to leave. They became abusive and refused to leave and further officers attended. All except the suspect then left. A WPC approached him and a scuffle broke out. He was eventually restrained with handcuffs and arrested.

Where violence towards the police was involved, it was fairly common for both section 5 and assault charges to be laid, either against the same individual or different participants. Indeed, nearly 40 per cent of this sub-group of cases involved section 5 and assault charges. The following is one example, involving fairly large-scale disorder and leading to three arrests.

> Huyton, case 19: the police had just carried out an arrest when a crowd of up to 40 people converged upon their vehicle, shouting and swearing at the officers. They attempted to open the van doors to release the prisoner. The first suspect, who appeared to be drunk, shouted: "that's my fucking nephew you twats have got in the car". He was warned to stop being abusive. He did not desist but became violent, striking the officer, and a struggle ensued.

During the course of this, he bit the officer on the arm. The second suspect then ran at the officers and shouted: "leave him alone you bastards or I'll fucking have you". He was warned to desist but he continued to be abusive. A third suspect then joined in the struggle, shouting: "there's not enough of you, you're all fucking dead". The first suspect was charged with ABH and drunk and disorderly, and the second and third suspects were charged with section 5 offences and obstruction.

Lastly, there was a small group of cases - 2 per cent of all cases - in which violence, initially between members of the public, was turned on the police when they intervened. An example is given below:

Durham case 136: the police were called to a disturbance in the city centre. The suspect was seen chasing another youth and throwing punches at him. A PC caught hold of the suspect who said: "fuck off, I'm going to kill the cunt". He struggled violently with the officer and they both fell to the ground. He was brought under control and warned that he would be arrested if he persisted. He continued with his threats to the other youth and was arrested. The police report notes that "about 20 to 30 people, including women, were around and observed what occurred".

Disorderly behaviour

Section 5 may encompass generally rowdy or disturbing behaviour that is liable to alarm members of the public, even though no specific threats or abuse are involved nor any violence. Thirteen per cent of incidents in the sample were so categorised. In two-thirds of these, the misconduct was akin to behaviour that could equally be termed 'drunk and disorderly' (the dividing line between section 5 offences and drunk and disorderly is variably drawn), while, in the remainder, there was no suggestion that the rowdy behaviour was influenced by drink. The first two examples given below fall into the first of these categories; in the third, drink was not involved.

Grimsby, case 96: the suspect, while apparently drunk, was observed trying to gain entry to an old peoples' home, claiming he wanted a glass of water. He was accompanied by a mongrel dog. Female staff and residents were frightened by his behaviour. He was subsequently found lying face down on the ground outside the home in the pouring rain. He was arrested.

Durham, case 38: the police were called to a large disturbance in the street, involving around 40 people at pub closing time on a Thursday night. The disturbance ceased when the police arrived and the crowd began to disperse. The suspect was seen shouting and was advised to refrain and go home. He refused and carried on shouting and was again advised to go home. He said to friends of his who were nearby: "take his fucking number, he can't tell anybody where to go". He was then arrested. Several local people had come out into the street because of the disturbance.

Huyton, case 29: the police were called to a college, where four males were creating a disturbance in the canteen and refusing to leave. When the police arrived, the men got up to go. One left a coat on a chair and one of the officers picked it up and asked whose it was. One of the youths turned and snatched it from him, saying: "it's not fucking yours, just give it to us". He was told to stop swearing but continued to do so. He refused to relinquish the coat and said: "you can't fucking search that". He was then arrested.

Indecency

One rather specific use of section 5 is in relation to some forms of indecent behaviour. These may be taken to fall within the category of 'insulting behaviour' encompassed by the section. Frequently, the behaviour in question amounted to urinating in view of passers-by, typically after licensed premises had closed on a Friday or Saturday night. In some areas, such as Durham, this was dealt with as the distinct offence of 'urination' under local bye-laws. But in other areas - and particularly Hull City and Grimsby - section 5 provided a useful means of dealing with this kind of behaviour. As in the following example, there was normally some kind of aggravating factor - such as abuse to the police or wilful exposure to passers-by - besides the actual urination to justify a section 5 arrest.

> Vine Street, case 356: the suspect approached patrolling police officers and asked where there was a toilet. They gave him some directions. He replied: "fuck that, I've just come from there. I'll piss somewhere else". One officer asked him where and he answered: "I'll piss where I want". The officer told him to make sure that it was in a public toilet. The suspect turned round, clenching his fists, shouted "fuck this" and stormed off. He was warned about his behaviour. He turned to friends who were with him and said: "I'll piss here when he's gone". He was warned not to by the officers. They started to walk away, but when they turned round they saw the suspect urinating against a wall. Pedestrians round about were "horrified and alarmed". He was arrested.

Section 5 was also used in situations where the indecency in question was of a sexual nature, as in the following two examples. In the first the behaviour consisted of indecent exposure and, in the second, to homosexual propositioning. Other provisions may not have been used in these and other cases for various reasons. The incidents may not have been serious enough, there may have been difficulties establishing the elements of the offences, there may not have been specific victims who came forward to give evidence, or victims may not have wished to proceed.

> Bristol City, case 237: the suspect was seen openly masturbating in a public car park while a female was passing by. Other members of the public were also using the carpark at the time. The police thereupon approached the suspect and arrested him under section 5.

> Hull City, case 46: a 14 year old boy was approached by the suspect outside a public toilet and propositioned. The suspect told the boy that he liked his "tight trousers" and asked him if he wanted to go "somewhere secret" to play pontoon. The boy told the police of the incident and the suspect was subsequently arrested.

Disorder associated with pubs or food outlets

Eight per cent of section 5 incidents were directly linked with licensed premises or take-away food outlets. Most frequently, the behaviour in question consisted of rowdy arguments or abuse which alarmed others using the premises in question or, where the incident occurred on the street outside, passers-by. The first of the incidents below was connected with licensed premises, while the second occurred at a restaurant.

> Bristol City, case 271: the police were called to a disturbance at a city centre pub at closing time on a Friday night. Two men had just been ejected by the doorman and one of them was heard swearing at him. The police warned him to stop and he replied: "fuck off, I'm not speaking to you, I'm speaking to that fucker". He was again asked to stop - several members of the public were in the vicinity. His friend took him away, swearing at the police: "you lot are a bunch of wankers, you think you're fucking hard". Shortly afterwards, the police saw him heading back towards the pub and he again began abusing the doorman. He was again warned and retorted: "I'm going to talk to that black fucker". He was arrested.

> Vine Street, case 203: the police were called to a disturbance at a restaurant late on a Friday night. Several people who were drunk, the suspect included, were ejected from the premises. As he was leaving he turned to a table of diners and shouted: "this place fucking sucks". They were "upset" by this remark. He was warned about his language, but repeated the abusive remark. He was arrested under section 5.

Domestic disputes

Use of section 5 is not generally appropriate in domestic disputes because arguments occurring in private dwellings that do not affect others outside do not fall within the section's ambit. Even where disputes occur in public or are in private but sufficiently vociferous to alarm those outside, the police may prefer to arrest using their common law powers to prevent a breach of the peace. However, in a small group of cases the police used section 5 to deal with what were essentially domestic disturbances, where these occurred in public or where they occurred in private but spilled over into public places. An example is given here:

> Huyton, case 68: a young woman had asked the police to help her retrieve some belongings from the marital home, as she was too scared of her husband to go there alone. Two officers went with her to assist. On their arrival, the husband came out into the garden waving a hammer and shouting: "the first one through this door gets this!" The officers called for assistance because they feared for their safety and because the woman was so scared that she would not leave the police car. The suspect continued to shout: "you can fuck off you little cunt - you've already taken my kid, now you've brought the heavy mob ...". On the arrival of help, the suspect was arrested for a section 5 offence.

HOME OFFICE RESEARCH STUDY No. 135

Football-related disorder
One minority use of section 5 was to deal with rowdiness associated with football supporters, usually, but not always, occurring at the grounds themselves. Some arrests were made where obscene chanting occurred and those taking part refused to desist when requested. Overall, 3 per cent of cases fell into this category, but several stations which had football grounds in their areas made far more use of section 5 in these circumstances. Thus, at Broadbury Road in Bristol, nearly one-quarter of section 5 arrests were connected with policing football supporters. The following are two typical examples, the first occurring at a football ground, the other elsewhere.

> Broadbury Road, case 319: the incident occurred in the family stand at a football stadium. The suspect was observed using obscene language when a woman with small children was sitting directly in front of him. He was warned but continued to be abusive, claiming when arrested that "I ain't fucking done nothing".

> Bristol City, case 191: a large group of football supporters marched on the city centre, waving their arms, shouting and singing. The suspect was leading the group, who had apparently been drinking. The group charged through the streets, shouting loudly and aggressively, causing shoppers to disperse. The suspect charged over the top of a parked car, causing the alarm to sound and damaging the car. He was then arrested by the police for a section 5 offence as well as for causing criminal damage.

Miscellaneous
The remaining 4 per cent of incidents reflect a range of different circumstances in which section 5 was employed. In a quarter of cases, arrests were made where the behaviour of suspects who had been taking drugs or, as in the next case, sniffing glue or other substances, alarmed passers-by.

> Vine Street, case 194: the suspect was seen by the police sitting in a shop doorway sniffing lighter fuel and shouting at passing pedestrians. He was heard to shout at one female: "what are you fucking looking at?" She appeared upset by this and the suspect was approached by the police and warned. He was then abusive and shouted: "I can't fucking stop, leave me alone". He started to shout again and attempted to retrieve the lighter fuel from the police. He was then arrested.

Arrests were made in other cases for a variety of reasons. There were some instances of sexual harassment in which section 5 was called upon, as in the following case.

> Hammersmith, case 96: the police were called to an office after the suspect, who was not known to those working there, had come into the premises and asked to use the toilet. This was refused. He then offered to help move some office equipment, and this was again refused. He was then seen to stand with his hands thrust into his pockets, "trying to arouse himself". The police told him to go away as women were upset by his behaviour. He then left. Shortly afterwards, one of the women from the office was conscious of the suspect walking quickly behind her as she left work and she called a nearby police officer. The suspect was arrested.

CLASSIFICATION OF OFFENSIVE CONDUCT

Variations in the use of section 5

There were three main variations between stations in the way section 5 was employed, as well as some lesser differences. While to some extent these would appear to reflect differences in the types of disorder occurring in specific areas, interviews with officers indicated that they also reflect varying views about the circumstances in which it is appropriate to arrest for section 5 offences. The differences principally concern: whether it is appropriate to arrest when the police are the victim; whether section 5 encompasses violent behaviour; and how section 5 is perceived as relating to or overlapping with other public order legislation.

Arrests where the police are victims
The extent to which the police are the targets of offensive conduct is considered in Chapter 5. Here the issue examined is differences in practice in making arrests in such cases. Of the incidents in the classification used above, a total of 44 per cent consisted, in essence, of abuse, threats or violence which were directed primarily at the police or at police and public jointly. However, at individual stations the proportion of arrests for 'police-oriented' offensive conduct differed very sharply. At the top of the range, over three-quarters of section 5 arrests at Kirkby and 70 per cent at Huyton were for such behaviour, compared with only 7 per cent at Grimsby, 14 per cent at Hull and one-third at Durham.

These differences may reflect that the police are abused far more in Huyton and Kirkby, and the evidence from speaking to officers in these areas is that relations with some sectors of the community are particularly bad here. However, the survey of patrol officers and those in Administrative Support Units also suggests that there is a real difference in police practice in making arrests where the police are the primary targets of abuse. Despite the ruling in the case of *D.P.P. v. Orum*[2] that section 5 does not preclude the possibility that police officers may be persons who are caused harassment, alarm or distress, officers in Hull particularly and at some other stations expressed doubts about magistrates' preparedness to accept that this could be so and this affected arrest practice in cases where they were subject to abuse. Officers at Hull and Durham also mentioned what they perceived as an unwillingness on the part of the CPS to take on cases where the police are the principal victim. (CPS decisions are, in fact, based on a review of the sufficiency of the evidence and an evaluation of whether prosecution is in the public interest - see Chapter 6.) These reservations on the part of the police did not necessarily mean that they would take no action where they came in for abuse. At Grimsby, for example, there was a high incidence of arrest to prevent a breach of the peace in such circumstances. At Huyton and Kirkby officers had no such reservations about the use of section 5 and would use it where they were the targets of particularly flagrant abuse or threats.

Violent behaviour and section 5 offences
It was noted above that the wording of section 5 does not contemplate the coverage of violent behaviour. However, there may be various reasons why some violent conduct

---
[2] *D.P.P.v. Orum* (1988), The Times, July 25. It was noted, however, that conduct which might cause harassment, alarm or distress to a member of the public might not have that effect on a police officer. See Chapter 5.

does become the subject of section 5 charges: for example, where the violence is minor or the victim is unprepared to press assault charges. The extent to which essentially violent incidents were subsumed under section 5 varied: while such cases on average constituted 13 per cent of section 5 offences, the proportion was as high as 27 per cent at Darlington and 21 per cent at Bristol compared with just 7 per cent at Grimsby and Hull.

One possibility considered was whether in areas where section 5 charges were brought in violence cases, assault charges were also brought. Is there in effect a 'loading on' of charges – the assault charge to cover the violent behaviour and the section 5 charge to cater for its likely impact on others? The converse of this is that in areas where section 5 was seldom used for violent behaviour, it might be expected that there would be greater economy of charges. In other words, police decisions about the appropriate charges would depend on the most important aspect of the incident: if this was the physical harm caused, assault charges might be brought, but if it was the alarm caused to others and the harm was trivial, section 5 might be used.

There was some evidence to support this view. Thus, at Bristol and Darlington, both section 5 and assault charges were brought in relation to 40 per cent and 25 per cent of violent incidents respectively. At Hull and Grimsby assault charges were hardly ever brought in conjunction with section 5 charges. It may be that these variations in practice reflect the robustness with which the police in different areas tackle the maintenance of public order. Where section 5 alone is used to deal with minor violence, this may reflect a view that particular kinds of violence - particularly that between youths who have been drinking on a Friday and Saturday night - are commonplace and amount to little more than 'disorderly behaviour' falling within the ambit of section 5. Where both assault and section 5 charges are brought, this may reflect that the actual level of violence is more serious. But it could also point to a firm stance on disorder which stresses not only the physical harm resulting from violence but also its wider impact on the public. More practically, another possibility is that section 5 charges were sometimes brought in conjunction with assault charges as a 'fail-safe' mechanism. Thus, if the assault charges were dropped, there would still be the section 5 offence to fall back upon.

Interface between section 5 and other public order law
Section 5 was introduced to deal with the specific problem of anti-social behaviour that disturbs members of the public but which had not hitherto been adequately caught by the criminal law. However, the breadth of the wording of this section means that it may capture misbehaviour covered by other provisions. A large majority of the officers interviewed for the study agreed that there were circumstances in which it was equally open to them to make an arrest under section 5 of the Public Order Act or under some other provision. Of those who had policing experience dating back to pre-Public Order Act days, over 80 per cent said that they would now sometimes use section 5 to make an arrest in circumstances where they would previously have used a pre-existing power.

The principal overlap is with behaviour that may constitute an offence contrary to section 91 of the Criminal Justice Act 1967 (drunk and disorderly) and with behaviour liable to cause a common law breach of the peace. There may also be grey areas between section 5 offences and misbehaviour falling within section 4 of the Public Order Act (fear or provocation of violence). Indeed, section 4 charges are frequently varied to section 5 by the Crown Prosecution Service. Additionally, behaviour that amounts to minor or technical assault or to indecency could sometimes be construed as falling within section 5.

These difficulties in distinguishing between the boundaries of different offences are manifest in certain differences between stations in the use of section 5 and other public order provisions (see Table 3.2 on page 20). To some extent these reflect the varying nature of disorder between areas, but some differences are so marked that this explanation cannot alone suffice. Interviews with police officers confirm differences in practice. Among the most notable is the wide variation in the contribution to public order offences of the offence of being drunk and disorderly: at several city/town centre stations in areas where drunkenness offences are known to be a problem, this offence contributed well below average proportions of public order arrests. Thus, there were relatively few such arrests at Hull, Durham and Darlington. On the other hand, section 5 contributed a large proportion of public order arrests at these stations. At Hull, officers interviewed pointed out that section 5 was actively preferred to drunk and disorderly, even for quite minor incidents of disorderliness. They pointed out that there were no agreed standards for evaluating what amounted to drunk and disorderly and section 5 offences. Opting for the latter had certain perceived advantages: it was seen as more of a deterrent as the offender was likely to be put before the court; courts took the offence more seriously; and there was no need to prove drunkenness.

Another variation is shown by Grimsby. There, hardly any arrests were made for drunk and disorderly, but the level of section 5 arrests was also below average. Instead, breach of the peace was frequently used where rowdy drunks created disturbances. Officers interviewed ascribed this practice to tradition that had remained largely unaffected by the advent of the Public Order Act. In the same force, a peculiarity of section 5 arrests at Hull was the presence of a sizeable minority of cases of urinating in the street. At most other stations, this conduct was variously dealt with under local by-laws or as drunk and disorderly behaviour.

Other variations are less apparent from Table 3.2 but were pointed out during the interview survey. At Huyton and Kirkby, for example, the drunk and disorderly category includes a range of behaviour, such as fighting, shouting abuse and kicking over dustbins, that elsewhere might have been diverted into section 5 or section 4 offences. Section 5 was relatively well used at these stations, but not as much as might have been expected given the nature of disorder locally, and section 4 was used hardly at all. The view of Huyton and Kirkby officers was that the bulk of disorder was related to drink and therefore drunk and disorderly was the appropriate charge. As one officer put it, to bring conduct within the Public Order Act, there would have to be "real violence", and to justify a section 4 charge someone would need to be receiving a "life-threatening pasting".

HOME OFFICE RESEARCH STUDY No. 135

Table 3.2: Section 5 and other public order arrests

Station	POA s.5 %	D&D %	D&I %	POA s.4 %	B of P'ce %	ABH As't %	Oth %
Hull Central	36	6	12	9	4	27	6
Durham	28	10	-	10	15	25	12
Huyton	27	18	-	-	20	30	5
Kirkby	26	31	-	2	12	18	11
Darlington	26	11	3	11	11	30	8
Derby	15	8	5	14	15	30	13
Vine Street	14	30	23	3	1	7	22
Broadbury Road	13	6	2	5	19	35	20
Grimsby	10	1	12	5	28	37	7
Hammersmith	7	19	38	5	3	18	10
Bristol Central	7	11	7	11	11	36	17
Total	**16**	**18**	**16**	**6**	**9**	**21**	**14**

Notes:
1. N = 2557.
2. 'D&I' is an abbreviation of drunk and incapable.
3. 'ABH/As't' includes assault occasioning actual bodily harm, common assault and assault on police.
4. 'Oth' includes sections 2 and 3 of the POA (violent disorder and affray - 1 per cent and 2 per cent of cases respectively), GBH (4 per cent of cases) and Obstruction (7 per cent of cases).

At some other stations it would appear from officers' comments that lower tolerance levels of disorder existed. (This point also comes out in the previous section, which points to differences in the extent to which section 5 incidents involved violence.) Perhaps the most notable example is Hull, where officers needed little encouragement to use section 5 as a means of controlling loud and high-spirited behaviour. In these circumstances, section 5 arrests were regarded very much as a preventive measure, in the way that arrests to prevent a breach of the peace were at some other stations.

These variations confirm the picture of the use of section 5 presented by the earlier Home Office research, that it is a flexible measure which is employed in a range of different situations (Newburn et al, 1991). That research examined just two forces. The present research, with its more widely drawn sample, suggests that there is a considerable lack of uniformity across the country as a whole in the way section 5 is interpreted and implemented. These variations arise for a variety of reasons. Pre-POA practice is one: hence the continued use of breach of the peace in some areas. It was also suggested by some officers that section 5 is regarded as analogous to section 5 of the 1936 Public

Order Act, and therefore sometimes applied in more serious situations than was the intent behind the legislation. The attitude of supervisors is another influence on officers' actions and may affect the choice of arrest provision. Instances were cited at stations where section 5 was 'popular' of grounds for detention being varied from drunk and disorderly to section 5, for example.

Different interpretations of the kind of behaviour with which the Act was intended to deal are another factor. It was noted above that a large majority of officers with beat experience prior to the introduction of the 1986 Act considered that section 5 could be used to deal with behaviour already covered by other provisions. However, they were almost equally split in their views about whether section 5 could be used to deal with misbehaviour that was not previously within the sphere of the criminal law (as indeed was one aim of the legislation). Those who considered section 5 had not really provided them with any extra power to arrest argued that, in the past, they would always have found a means to arrest if misbehaviour was sufficiently offensive.

Also relevant is the perceived reaction to section 5 charges of the CPS and the courts. (The outcome of section 5 charges is dealt with in chapter 6.) This could affect the extent to which section 5 was used in preference to other provisions, as well as the kinds of misbehaviour to which it was applied, particularly where the issue arose of whether the police could be regarded as the victim.

Beliefs and opinions among the police about the appropriateness of particular public order provisions to particular situations are something which become part of the culture of individual stations. Officers mutually reinforce each others views about when it is 'correct' to arrest for drunk and disorderly and when section 5 may be used, for example. Such shared 'cultural' understandings may be significantly affected by the views of custody officers. These varying local interpretations are fostered by the lack of any coherent national or force-wide guidance about the situations in which different public order provisions should be used. The overwhelming majority of officers interviewed indicated that no such instructions were issued either centrally by their forces or by the CPS. The views of the police at station level about the use of public order law are not necessarily 'wrong'. As has been observed elsewhere, the law is essentially permissive of such variations (McBarnet, 1981). Whether these differences in practice are desirable is another matter, an important consideration here being that the outcome for the suspect may differ according to the offence for which he or she is arrested.

HOME OFFICE RESEARCH STUDY No. 135

4 The circumstances of offences

Previous research on the Public Order Act has suggested that offences of disorder follow very specific patterns: for example, in terms of who commits them, and when and where (Newburn et al, 1991). The present research suggests that the low level disorderly situations covered by section 5 are no exception. Information about the situational context of offences is considered in this chapter. As well as looking at the time and place of offences and those who committed them, it considers whether alcohol was involved and the extent to which race was a factor.

Location

Table 4.1 shows that section 5 offences most frequently occurred in the street. This is unsurprising in view of the drafting of the section, which does not encompass behaviour occurring in a dwelling (except where it affects persons outside). A significant minority of offences (15 per cent) were linked with licensed premises (public houses or night-clubs), and either occurred within those premises or took the form of brawls or arguments that originated inside but spilled out onto the street.

Clustering of offences at other locations reflects situational aspects of disorder in town and city centres (Ramsay, 1982; Wood and Goodall, n.d.). For example, minorities of incidents occurred at restaurants and takeaways or were associated with public transport. The 10 per cent of incidents occurring at 'public premises' included disturbances at locations such as the public areas of hospitals, police stations and social security offices, and public parks.

The six per cent of incidents listed as occurring at dwellings were largely domestic or inter-neighbour disputes which took place out on the street or in gardens or occurred indoors but were sufficently rowdy to alarm passers-by.

Table 4.1: Location of section 5 offences

Location	N cases	%
Street	427	49
In/near licensed premises	133	15
Public premises/parks/open spaces	91	10
Shops/commercial premises	74	8
Private dwelling	53	6
Public transport/car/taxi	46	5
Restaurant/takeaway	41	5
In/near football ground	16	2
Total	881	100

The significance of particular types of location varied somewhat between stations. This may in part have reflected differences in the nature of the areas policed. But it probably also reflected differences in the way the police used section 5 (see previous chapter). Among the more notable differences in the location of incidents were the following. Street incidents constituted two-thirds of cases at Vine Street, a station which covered an area of the West End of London where the streets are busy with people intent on entertainment. At Hammersmith, nearly a quarter of incidents were associated with locations classified as 'public premises', and included disturbances at Hammersmith Hospital, the police station itself, a hostel for the homeless and a cemetery.

A feature of some areas was the extent of disorder associated with licensed premises. Over a third of incidents at Darlington and around a quarter at Derby and at Hull fell into this category. In these areas, more so than in the South, Friday and Saturday nights are a time for going out, and the hectic level of activity in pubs and clubs late in the evening creates the potential for disorder. The level of section 5 arrests at these locations may also have reflected localised police preferences for using this section rather than arresting for drunk and disorderly or taking action short of arrest (see Chapter 3).

One further feature of note was the use of section 5 in cases involving various kinds of disorder by football supporters at Broadbury Road. Nearly a quarter of cases in which section 5 was used fell into this category here. And, lastly, significant minorities of cases at Huyton (19 per cent) and Kirkby (13 per cent) were associated with private dwellings. This reflected the residential nature of these areas and that section 5, rather than breach of the peace, was sometimes used to cope with domestic disputes that had a public element.

Timing

Incidents leading to section 5 arrests followed distinct patterns in terms of time of day and day of week. Predominating was a trend for disorder to occur during the late evening and early hours of the morning at weekends, suggesting that leisure time revelry that sometimes gets out of hand is at the root of many incidents. Of all cases in the sample, 60 per cent occurred on Friday and Saturday[1] and the 30 hours between 2100 on a Friday and 0300 on Sunday morning accounted for no less than 43 per cent of all incidents (see Table 4.2).

The significance of the weekend as the occasion for disorder varied between areas, broadly reflecting the differences noted in the previous section in the extent to which Friday and Saturday were the focus for the week's social activity and in the nature of the area policed. Table 4.2 shows that well over half of all section 5 offences occurred in the 30 hour period that is the core of the social weekend at Derby, Darlington and Hull. In London, where social activity tends to be spread more evenly through the week, the level of disorder at the weekend was not noticeably higher than at other times. In some areas which did not contain centres that attracted large crowds at the weekend - for example, Kirkby and Huyton - weekend levels of disorder were again low.

---

[1] Each day is taken as running from 0300 to 0259 to follow more closely the pattern of social activity and, particularly, to avoid an unnatural midnight cut-off point between Saturday and Sunday.

Table 4.2: Time of section 5 offences

Station	Weekday %	Weekend %
Durham	51	49
Darlington	41	59
Hammersmith	65	35
Vine Street	69	31
Huyton	80	20
Kirkby	72	28
Hull Central	44	56
Grimsby	64	36
Bristol Central	62	38
Broadbury Road	59	41
Derby	40	60
Total	57	43

NOTES:
1. N = 867. Details about time were missing for 14 cases.
2. Weekend = 2100 Friday to 0259 Sunday.

The presence of alcohol

In 44 per cent of section 5 offences, the suspects arrested were known to have been drinking beforehand.[2] It is not possible to say to what extent alcohol was a contributory factor to offensive behaviour; however, the frequency with which it was present suggests the link. There is no doubt that the police involved in making arrests intended this inference to be drawn, for their accounts often made explicit references to the fact that suspects appeared to be the worse for wear through drink. The following is one example:

> Hammersmith, case 183: following an earlier incident, the two suspects in this case were seen in the early hours of a Saturday morning shouting and swearing and running in and out of the road. They entered a minicab office and were observed jostling and arguing with staff. The police asked them to leave. They became aggressive and abusive towards the officers and walked off still swearing. They then saw a police van, which contained a person who had been arrested, and the two suspects walked over to it and continued to shout abuse at the police. They were warned and then arrested. Police notes of the incident state that both men had been drinking.

Where the offending behaviour amounts to little more than general disorderliness, the police have the option of arresting for drunk and disorderly under section 91 of the Criminal Justice Act 1967. Not surprisingly, therefore, relatively few of the cases involving alcohol and leading to section 5 arrests amounted to disorderliness pure and simple. There was normally some other element present, such as the threat of violence or indecent exposure, which would be likely in the view of the police to alarm or distress members of the public. Cases involving alcohol therefore spanned the various classifications of offences outlined in the previous chapter.

---

[2] The proportion of cases in which suspects had been drinking is probably considerably higher than this: in 35 per cent of cases, over half of which occurred towards the end of or after licensing hours, no information on alcohol consumption was available.

HOME OFFICE RESEARCH STUDY No. 135

There were particularly heavy concentrations of alcohol related offences at specific stations. This reflected patterns of social behaviour already decribed, involving socialising and heavy drinking at the weekend and leading to hectic and chaotic scenes in town and city centres when licensed premises closed. Thus, no less than three-quarters of all section 5 arrests in Darlington and Hull were alcohol related, and Durham, Grimsby, Derby and Bristol Central all had well above average levels of arrests for offences in which alcohol was implicated. Those arrested for section 5 offences were often a few identifiable participants from large groups involved in major disturbances in which alcohol clearly played a part. One example of the confused circumstances in which such incidents occurred is given here.

> Durham, case 160: just after midnight on a Saturday night, an argument developed among a group of about 20 youths who had just emerged from a nightclub. They ranged themselves into two factions and a considerable amount of abuse was hurled between them. The police arrived at this point and warned them to quieten down and to move on. One shouted at the police: "Fuck off you black cunts", and was arrested, struggling violently. A second youth then intervened and tried to pull the police away, punching out towards them. He too was arrested. The arrests were the signal for pandemonium to break out, and a number of females were running to and fro among the police screaming abuse. The first youth arrested was still causing problems and he and the officer holding onto him fell against a car, smashing a window. A third youth was hit by a police truncheon, which led to a fourth one coming to his assistance. Meanwhile, two other youths had started to fight each other, leading to police intervention and further threats from the youths. Throughout the incidents, others on the periphery were kicking and punching at the police. Ten officers were involved and six arrests were made under sections 4 and 5 of the POA and for obstruction.

The offenders

Age and sex

From the nature of the incidents described, it is little surprise that the great majority of offenders were young males. Around 90 per cent were male and this figure varied little between stations. Nearly two-thirds were aged 24 or under, and it is probably no coincidence that it is this age group which previous Home Office research has shown to be particularly prone to involvement in drinking related disorder (Tuck, 1989). In some areas, the proportion of offenders in this age group was even higher, reaching a maximum of 80 per cent in Kirkby and Huyton. However, these statistics do not serve only to point up the prevalence of drink related disorder among the young. By no means all incidents were drink related and the figures also point to the degree to which anti-police and anti-social attitudes among some young people are manifested in misbehaviour which causes alarm to both police and public.

THE CIRCUMSTANCES OF OFFENCES

The average age of those arrested was 25 years. This figure is skewed by the involvement in a minority of offences of older offenders. Nearly 10 per cent were aged over 40 years. This serves as a reminder that section 5 may embrace a wider variety of conduct than drink related disorder in town centres. Those involved in some other kinds of incident - for example, domestic disputes - were often older.

Employment and criminal record

Forty per cent of section 5 offenders were unemployed, 50 per cent were in employment, while the remainder were students or housewives. There were variations between stations in the proportion employed. This partly reflected regional differences in rates of unemployment: thus 60 per cent or more of offenders were unemployed at Huyton and Kirkby in Merseyside. Where the nature of disorder was primarily city centre, alcohol-related disturbances, there was a tendency for the proportion of offenders employed to be higher. Thus, at Darlington the employment rate was 70 per cent and at Derby 60 per cent. This may reflect that those who can afford to spend money on alcohol and entertainment are more likely to be those in employment (Tuck, 1989; Field, 1990).

Two-thirds of section 5 offenders had criminal records[3] and, of this group, two-fifths had previous convictions that included one or more public order related offences, ranging from drunk and disorderly up to violent disorder. In all, a quarter of section 5 offenders had prior public order convictions. In some areas, the proportion was considerably higher. Thus, the percentage of section 5 offenders with prior public order convictions was 65 per cent in Grimsby, 54 per cent at Darlington and 40 per cent at Hull. It is not possible to say whether these variations reflect greater involvement in public disorder of some members of the population in specific areas or stricter police enforcement of the public order laws. Another possibility is that differences in prosecution policy may play a part. Cautions will not show up in statistics on previous convictions, nor will bind overs without a finding of guilt (see Chapter 6).

Others involved

Incidents leading to section 5 charges sometimes involved other participants who were charged with different offences. This occurred in six per cent of cases (55 out of 881). Most frequently, other participants were charged under section 4 of the Public Order Act 1986 (fear or provocation of violence - in 21 cases), with obstructing the police (12 cases), assault (11 cases) or being drunk and disorderly (10 cases). Section 5 cases also sometimes involved participants (victims aside) who were arrested but not proceeded against. In seven per cent of cases, other suspects were released without any further action.

Mention should also be made of the fact that many incidents involved persons who participated in offensive conduct or were on the periphery of it but were not arrested. It was sometimes physically not possible for the police to arrest more than a few main offenders and others made good their escape. Police reports allow some assessment to be made of the scale of others' involvement. These suggest that, in over a third of cases, persons other than those arrested were associated with the offensive behaviour. Roughly half of these may be categorised as small-scale incidents in which only one or two others

---

[3]Information about criminal record was not available for a quarter of offenders. These percentages are based on those for whom previous conviction data were available.

were not captured. But about 40 per cent were large-scale incidents in which five or more (sometimes very many more) participants were not detained.

Race

Smith (1987) has noted that the breadth of the language used in the drafting of section 5 allows considerable scope for "injudicious" policing. He draws attention to the danger that section 5 might lead to the criminalisation of conduct that amounts to little more than arguing with a police officer. There was indeed patent apprehension on the part of the Government about creating legislation that might be too similar to the discredited 'sus' laws.[4] Stevens and Willis (1979) note that a particular feature of those laws was their disproportionate use against black people.[5] In the Metropolitan Police, 1975 data showed that 40 per cent of 'sus' arrests were of black people, yet members of this group made up only 4 per cent of the population.

Representation of ethnic minorities among section 5 offenders
Police records do not always contain information on ethnicity and this limited the extent to which this issue could be considered in the present study. However, sufficient data were available to draw some tentative conclusions about the representation of ethnic minorities among section 5 offenders. First of all, data on ethnicity were available from custody records for the two Metropolitan Police stations (Hammersmith and Vine Street), thus providing some indication of the representation of minority groups among those **arrested** for section 5 offences. Secondly, complete data on ethnicity were available at the same two stations and incomplete data at five more for those **proceeded against**. Thirdly, to explore whether the representation of ethnic minorities in section 5 cases differed from other types of case, data on ethnicity were also extracted from samples of custody records and case files for other offences. The offences sampled were broadly within the compass of public order, ranging from assault occasioning grievous bodily harm down to drunk and disorderly.

There are difficulties interpreting the data, one being the lack of accurate information about the ethnic minority population of the areas covered by the stations. While data from the 1991 Census are now available (OPCS, 1993), as well as information from the annually conducted Labour Force Survey (Haskey, 1991), with the exception of Hammersmith the areas used as the basis for estimates are too large for them to be directly useful for the purposes of the present study. A difficulty at two stations in particular - Vine Street in the West End of London and Bristol Central - is that local population estimates have little relevance since a high, but unknown, proportion of people on the streets will not live locally but will have travelled to the area for work or pleasure.

Any interpretation must also bear in mind significant differences in the age structure of ethnic minority groups. Most notably, those in the age range most prone to offend are over-represented among Afro-Caribbeans and Asians (Indian, Pakistani and Bangladeshi), with 29 per cent and 25 per cent respectively of these groups falling into the 16 to 29 age bracket compared with 21 per cent of white people (OPCS, 1992).

---

[4] Section 4 of the Vagrancy Act 1824 created the offence of being a suspected person loitering with intent to commit an arrestable offence. This was abolished by section 8 of the Criminal Attempts Act 1981.
[5] Stevens and Willis use the term 'black' to refer to black-skinned West Indian or African people. Elsewhere in this report the term 'Afro-Caribbean' is generally used.

Partly because of these difficulties, figures on the proportion of ethnic minority suspects involved in section 5 offences must be treated with some caution. Additionally, it should be noted that, while the study collected arrest data for a three month period, the samples of section 5 offences obtained were quite small, both overall and compared with other public order offences (see Table 2.3 in Chapter 2).

At Hammersmith and Vine Street, the two stations for which usable ethnic data on arrests were obtained, there were, respectively, totals of 26 and 106 section 5 arrests during the research, compared with 372 and 723 other public order arrests. The small samples mean that the range of uncertainty surrounding the proportion of ethnic minority arrests is quite high.[6]

At Hammersmith 27 per cent (+/-18 per cent) and at Vine Street 12 per cent (+/- 6 per cent) of those arrested for section 5 offences were Afro-Caribbeans. These figures may be compared with data from the 1991 Census on the ethnic mix of areas. These show that the proportion of Afro-Caribbean residents numbers just over 10 per cent in Hammersmith (OPCS, 1993). The population figures for Vine Street are more problematic because the area has a large transient population. There is probably little value in using population figures for the whole of Greater London as a yardstick,[7] since the ethnic breakdown of the floating population of the Vine Street area may bear little relationship to that of London in general. On the face of it, therefore, the most that can be said is that there appears to be some over-representation of Afro-Caribbeans among those arrested for section 5 offences in Hammersmith. However, bearing in mind the uncertainty levels surrounding these figures and the point noted earlier that a higher proportion of Afro-Caribbeans than whites fall in the 16-29 age range, it is doubtful whether these figures do in fact point conclusively to the over-representation of Afro-Caribbeans in the section 5 arrest population.

The examination of other (ie. non-section 5) public order arrests showed that the proportion of Afro-Caribbeans arrested for these offences was lower than that found in section 5 cases. The respective figures were 9 per cent and 6 per cent at Hammersmith and Vine Street. These are closer to what might be expected from the population estimates provided above. Bearing in mind that these figures are based on larger samples than those available for section 5 arrests (over 1,000 non-section 5 arrests were examined), the likelihood must be considered that the ethnic imbalance in the sample of section 5 arrests is due to chance rather than to any kind of discriminatory policing.

Asians formed only a small proportion of those arrested for either section 5 or other public order offences at Hammersmith and Vine Street. At Hammersmith, they comprised 4 per cent of section 5 suspects - identical to the proportion of Asians in the local population (Haskey, 1991). At Vine Street only 1 per cent were Asians. This is possibly a lower figure than might have been expected; however, without reliable statistics on the proportion of Asians in the area covered by Vine Street police,[8] no firm conclusions can be drawn as to whether this group are genuinely under-represented

---

[6] The confidence limits around the percentages at Hammersmith are +/-18% and at Vine Street +/-6%, both at the 95% confidence level.
[7] Census data show that Afro-Caribbeans make up around 8% of the Greater London population (OPCS, 1993).

among section 5 suspects. It must also be kept in mind that, as with the arrest figures for Afro-Caribbeans, the figures for Asians are also subject to the same wide margins of error and that variations due to chance may explain the relatively low number of arrests among this group.

There is some evidence from the arrest data that proceedings followed arrest less frequently in the case of Afro-Caribbean suspects, although numbers are again too small to allow firm conclusions to be drawn. At Hammersmith and Vine Street (the only two stations for which this information was available) nearly all of 112 white suspects were charged, cautioned or summonsed compared with 85 per cent of the 20 Afro-Caribbeans in the sample at these stations (not a statistically significant difference). The differential rate of proceeding was not confined to section 5 cases: in the range of other disorderly offences, the respective rates of charging, cautioning or summonsing white and Afro-Caribbean suspects were 92 per cent and 81 per cent. These differences were not accounted for by police reluctance to proceed against young offenders: very few of either white or Afro-Caribbean suspects in public order cases were aged under 17.

Turning to those proceeded against, the case file sample provides some data on ethnicity from a wider range of stations than the arrest sample (seven in all), although complete data are only to be found for the two London stations. Of nearly 1,200 suspects proceeded against for section 5 offences at the seven stations, just over 6 per cent were known to be Afro-Caribbeans. It is likely that this marks an over-representation of this group, which forms only around 1 per cent of the country's population. However, as noted earlier, the difficulty is of relating this information to data at the level of areas covered by police stations on the distribution of ethnic minority groups. The exception is Hammersmith, where estimates of the ethnic minority population are available. Here, just over a fifth of those proceeded against for section 5 offences were Afro-Caribbeans (23 out of 112), but this group comprised 10 per cent of the local population. Taking into account the range of uncertainty (+/- 8 per cent) attached to these figures due to the small sample size, there still appears to be some over-representation of Afro-Caribbeans.

Differences in the age structure of the Afro-Caribbean population do not account for their higher than anticipated presence among section 5 offenders. In fact, fewer than expected were found in the 16 to 29 age group. Only two-thirds of Afro-Caribbeans proceeded against for section 5 offences fell into this age bracket compared with just over three-quarters of white offenders. Afro-Caribbeans were in fact over-represented in the older age groups: one-third were aged 30 or over, compared with one-fifth of whites.

There was some slight evidence that the over-representation of Afro-Caribbeans among section 5 defendants was greater than for other kinds of public order offences. Data from seven stations in the case file sample showed that 5 per cent (+/- 1%) of those proceeded against for other offences were known to be Afro-Caribbeans (96 out of 1800) in contrast with 6 per cent (+/- 1.5%) of section 5 defendants (61 out of 974). However, the difference is too small and the amount of missing data on ethnicity too great[9] to allow any firm conclusions to be drawn from this.

---

[8]The latest census data show that Asians constitute around 7 per cent of the Greater London population (OPCS, 1993).

THE CIRCUMSTANCES OF OFFENCES

The data collected for this study suggest that it may be prudent to examine the issue of ethnicity and use of section 5 further before reaching any conclusions about whether there is any bias in the way the provision is applied or in decisions about proceedings. Certainly, the evidence to support any such accusation is not as acute as was the case with the former 'sus' laws (see above). To explore the use of section 5 in relation to black people in more depth would require more detailed study of police practice at street level. Although some observation of public order policing was undertaken for the present study, it was not systematic or lengthy enough to indicate whether there is any bias in the application of the law. Certainly, no overt examples of discrimination were observed during the course of the fieldwork.

The racial dimension in section 5 cases

Members of ethnic minorities were known to have been involved in 75 cases in which section 5 charges were laid. Of these, there was a racial dimension in 20, in the sense that explicit reference was made to race or ethnicity in police accounts, and that race appeared to have some bearing on the nature of the incident. All these cases involved Afro-Caribbeans. In a further 16, there was some suspicion that race may have been relevant but police accounts of events are not conclusive. In the remainder, there was no evidence either way that race was a factor in the incident. Examples from the first two groups of cases are given below. The cases appear to reflect perceptions by Afro-Caribbeans' that police action was discriminatory. Whether these perceptions were justified cannot be established since there is no evidence other than police accounts of incidents on which to draw. However, on the face of it, the facts as reported do not suggest anything improper in the actions of the police. There is equally the possibility that discrimination was raised by those arrested as a defence to counter police intervention, when in fact their behaviour was simply unacceptable.

The first three cases provide examples of police use of PACE stop and search powers which degenerated into situations in which an arrest under section 5 was considered necessary.

> Vine Street, case 171: the suspect was stopped by the police for a minor traffic offence and asked to get out of his car. He complied and, as he did so, said: "What's this about? I've done nothing wrong". The police told him to calm down but he became more irate. He apparently shouted: "This is not a free country if you're black - why are you harassing me?" He was again warned to calm down but continued to shout at the police officer. By this time a significant crowd had gathered. He was arrested for a section 5 offence.

> Hammersmith, case 231: two black males were stopped at 8.30 in the evening by the police, following a report of a burglary nearby. One of them said to the police: "No way, man, I haven't done anything - what are you trying to stitch me up with man?" The police tried to question

---

[9] Data on ethnicity were missing in around one-fifth of cases.

him but he was becoming more aggressive and abusive, retorting: "Fuck off man, I've done nothing". He was again told to calm down and apparently responded by grabbing hold of one PC's arms and pushing him away shouting: "Fuck off man, just harass someone else". He was then arrested.

Hammersmith, case 238: the police stopped the suspect, who was riding a mountain bicycle along the pavement. When asked why he was riding on the pavement he retorted: "It's none of your business". The police asked if the bicycle was his and he replied: "Fuck you, you've only stopped me because I'm black". He became increasingly abusive and was warned about his language. There were several passers-by at the time. The police told him that they wanted to do a check on his bicycle and he said: "Do what you fucking want, it's not stolen". He was again warned, replied "this is a fucking joke" and was arrested.

Stop and search cases aside, similar perceptions of racial bias ran through a number of other cases in which the police were involved in enforcing the law or keeping the peace.

Hammersmith, case 309: the suspect had attended a Job Centre and an altercation with a member of staff took place. The suspect refused to leave and the police were called. They asked what had happened and when the member of staff gave her version of events the suspect allegedly retorted: "You're a liar, white slag, a racist liar". He continued to shout abuse when removed from the premises. He was warned to stop, whereupon he rounded upon the police and said: "You can't tell me what to do, racist pig". He continued to be abusive. At the time the shopping centre was very busy. He was arrested.

Hammersmith, case 128: the police were called to a housing estate because of a disturbance involving youths throwing stones at younger children. One of the former, an Afro-Caribbean youth, was detained and the police asked him to take them to his parents' house. The boy struggled violently and made off. The police went after him to his house and asked to talk to his mother. She was apparently very abusive and refused to talk about the boy. During the course of an argument with the police, she allegedly poked one of them in the chest, and continually accused them of harassment. When warned to calm down she apparently retorted: "I don't fucking care, you're so fucking out of order. Fuck you, you're just filth". A crowd of around 30 people had gathered to watch. At this point she was arrested.

Two cases involving a number of suspects arose out of demonstrations about alleged police brutality against black people and unjustified arrests. One example is given below.

Hammersmith, case 177: a group of around 20 people had gathered at the police station to demonstrate about the arrest of black people, alleging police violence. They were gradually moved out of the police station, but one person refused to move and put his arms through the railings outside the station. He shouted: "Fuck off, I'm not moving till we get justice". He was told to move but shouted further abuse and waved his fist at a PC. After a further warning he was arrested following a violent struggle. Two other persons then joined in. One caught hold of an officer's tunic; the other was seized by the police and caught his head against the station door. He shouted: "Look what they're doing - brutality, police brutality!" All three were arrested (two under section 5 and one under section 4 of the POA).

One further theme to cases with racial overtones was apparently gratuitous abuse directed at the police in a few cases.

> Bristol Central, case 100: as the suspect passed a police officer he said: "Fuck off". The officer warned him not to swear. The suspect replied: "I will if I want to - fuck off". The officer asked him why he was swearing: "Because I don't like you, I don't like the police". He was warned again and further abuse followed, leading to his arrest. On arrest he said: "You can't arrest me for swearing, all the blacks do it. What is this, 'pick on a nigger' week?"

Further evidence that there was a specifically racial dimension to section 5 cases is obtained by examining incidents in terms of the categories outlined in Chapter 2. This analysis showed marked differences between Afro-Caribbean and white suspects; the pattern for Asians was also distinctly different. The essential difference for Afro-Caribbeans was that by far the largest proportion of incidents fell into the categories of abusive, threatening or violent behaviour directed at the police. No less than 48 per cent of section 5 incidents in which they were involved fell into these categories, compared with a figure of 28 per cent for white suspects. If incidents in which both police and public were targets of abuse or threats are also included, the difference between Afro-Caribbean and white suspects becomes even more marked, with respective figures of 69 per cent and 37 per cent. One worrying implication of these figures is that there is genuinely greater friction between black people and the police, which is readily manifested in hostile encounters in everyday policing situations. Various surveys have pointed to a lower level of trust in the police among Afro-Caribbeans and dissatisfaction with the way encounters are handled by the police (Field, 1984; Skogan, 1990; Southgate and Crisp, 1993). Given these tenuous relations, it may well be that black people are more likely to perceive section 5 warnings about their behaviour as provocation, leading to an escalation of the situation. Another possibility is that the police are more ready to react adversely where they receive abuse from black people. Without data on the extent to which the police tolerated abuse from white and black people respectively without taking steps to arrest no firm conclusions can be drawn in this respect.

HOME OFFICE RESEARCH STUDY No. 135

There is a particular problem in relation to stop and search. Afro-Caribbeans are more likely to be stopped by the police than white people and, thereafter, to be searched. This applies particularly to young Afro-Caribbean males (Smith, 1983; Skogan, 1990). Whether or not this represents discrimination or the valid application of the statutory grounds for stopping and searching is open to debate. However, it is undoubtedly the case that Afro-Caribbeans are prone to perceive bias in such contacts (Smith, 1983) and there is therefore a particular need for such encounters to be sensitively handled by the police if friction is to be avoided.

Incidents involving Asian suspects were essentially non-violent, and characterised by abuse directed at members of the public, normally following some kind of dispute or sometimes simply as a result of too much alcohol. Nearly 60 per cent of cases were categorised in this way, compared with 13 per cent for white people. Incidents of abuse or threats directed at the police were rare and the proportion far lower than for either whites or Afro-Caribbeans.

5 Victims of offensive conduct

Section 5 of the Public Order Act makes no requirement that offensive conduct be directed at anyone in order for the offence to be made out. There may well, as Smith (1987) notes, be someone present who is actually harassed, alarmed or distressed by the behaviour and this is all to the good because they may act as a witness. However, the evidence of a victim is not conclusive because it is enough that there is someone within sight or hearing who is **likely** to be caused harassment, alarm or distress. The judgement as to whether the conduct might have this effect is for the police and does not require a witness statement.

The Government White Paper, which proposed the present section 5 offence, had suggested that in order to make out the offence, substantial alarm, harassment or distress should actually have been caused (Home Office, 1985). The reason for doing so was concern that the ambit of the law might be too wide if it encompassed behaviour that was merely likely to cause alarm or distress. However, the White Paper's proposals presented difficulties. As Smith (1987) points out, securing evidence of the actual effect of offensive conduct points to the need for testimony from the victim. But the section was designed to protect precisely those vulnerable members of society who are unwilling to attend court for fear of reprisals. To overcome this obstacle, the prosecution are required only to testify that there was someone in the vicinity who was likely to have been harassed, alarmed or distressed.

Considerable debate has surrounded the question of whether police officers themselves may be victims of section 5 offences. Smith (*ibid*), in a commentary on the 1986 Act, expressed the view that there is no reason why policemen should not be regarded as victims of offensive conduct, although it might perhaps be more difficult to alarm them than the vulnerable persons whom the offence is principally designed to protect. However, another commentator, Thornton (1987), has suggested that a police officer should not be distressed by mere abuse or insulting behaviour and that it would be unlikely that an offence would have been committed if there was no-one within sight or hearing other than a police officer.

The issue was resolved at a fairly early stage when it was held in the case of *D.P.P. v. Orum*[1] that there was nothing in section 5 that led to the conclusion that a police officer might not be a person who was caused harassment, alarm or distress by the conduct to which the section applied. It was clearly recognised, however, that conduct which might cause harassment, alarm or distress to a member of the public might not have that effect on a police officer. Whether the behaviour had this effect was a question that depended on the facts of each case. Previously, the courts had relied on the decision in *Marsh v.*

---

[1]*D.P.P. v. Orum* (1988), The Times, July 25.

HOME OFFICE RESEARCH STUDY No. 135

Arscott[2] as authority to the contrary. However, as Birch (1988) points out in her note on the *Orum* case, *Marsh v. Arscott* was concerned with section 5 of the 1936 Public Order Act and the point at issue was whether a police officer who had been exposed to threatening, abusive or insulting words or behaviour was likely to react by breaching the peace. Not surprisingly, it was held that a police officer was unlikely to react in an unlawful way. Section 5 does not require such a reaction, but only the experiencing of alarm or distress.

In theory, therefore, the *Orum* case leaves the field open for police officers to arrest in situations in which they are occasioned alarm or distress and where they reasonably believe a section 5 offence has been committed. However, these situations must be distinguished from those where members of the public are treated as the victims. In the latter, actual alarm or distress need not necessarily have been caused; a likelihood is sufficient. In the former, logic dictates that alarm or distress must in fact have been caused to a police officer. As Birch (*ibid*) points out: "[i]f a quick psychoanalysis reveals that he is unmoved or even bored, he cannot arrest". The standard of offensive conduct that is sufficient will depend on the individual susceptibilities of the officer concerned. There is no need for any foresight on the part of the defendant that he or she might cause harassment, alarm or distress. It is only necessary to prove that the defendant was aware that his or her words or behaviour were abusive or insulting or that he or she intended them to be.

While it is settled that the police may be victims in section 5 cases, it is doubtful whether this development was contemplated when the legislation was introduced. Government proposals for the legislation cited a variety of instances of misbehaviour, not at that time readily susceptible to legal control, at which a low-level public order offence might be targeted (Home Office, 1985). A common element was the alarm caused to members of the public, particularly the more vulnerable. For example:

> "hooligans on housing estates causing disturbances in the common parts of blocks of flats, blockading entrances, throwing things down the stairs, banging on doors, peering in at windows, and knocking over dustbins; .... rowdy behaviour in the street late at night which alarms local residents".

The remainder of this chapter considers who, in practice, were the victims in section 5 offences.

The public as victims

In 80 per cent of cases (703 out of 881) police accounts suggested that members of the public were victims of offensive conduct for which section 5 arrests were made. In three-quarters of these cases (60 per cent of all cases), they were apparently the sole victims, while in 20 per cent (16 per cent of all cases) police officers were also apparently victims.

A distinction can be drawn between those cases in which there was some evidence that a member of the public had indeed suffered harassment, alarm or distress ('direct' victims)

---

[2] *Marsh v. Arscott* (1982), 75 Cr App R, 211.

VICTIMS OF OFFENSIVE CONDUCT

and those in which it was only inferred or implied by officers that this was a likely consequence of the suspect's conduct ('indirect' victims). The former were nearly twice as numerous as the latter, with police reports referring to evident alarm or distress in roughly two-thirds of cases in which members of the public were victims. In the remainder, police reports tended only to mention that there were passers-by or members of the public nearby, without providing any assessment of the effect of the offensive behaviour. As will be noted below, the presence of members of the public was a useful way of justifying police intervention in situations where the primary objective was probably to preserve respect for the police.

Often no particular person or persons were named as victims, even where it was a case of 'direct' victimisation. Indeed, section 5 does not require an identifiable victim or statements from victims for the offence to be made out. One rationale for this is that the police are acting on the community's behalf in maintaining the peace. It is relevant in this regard to note that in 70 per cent of section 5 offences the police intervened of their own accord without a complaint having been made by a member of the public. A further justification for not requiring a specified victim is that it is in the public interest that vulnerable members of society, who may fear reprisals, should not have to come forward to give evidence in court.

'Direct' victimisation

The following case, in which members of the public were the targets of hooligan behaviour, illustrates very well the kind of circumstances with which section 5 was designed to deal.

> Hammersmith, case 174: following public complaints about groups of youths using a cemetery as a drinking place, surveillance was mounted. A group of six youths was observed shouting and swearing at passers-by and drinking from a large bottle of vodka. One of the group threw a stick at one passer-by and it hit him. He turned round but before he could say anything, one of the group of youths walked towards him shouting: "what's your fucking game ... what's your fucking problem?" He returned to the bench and the youths continued to shout at passers-by. They also made masturbating gestures at one female. All were arrested.

Section 5 charges were also sometimes brought where the behaviour went beyond the insulting or threatening and actually involved violence. The following is one of many examples.

> Vine Street, case 158: the police intervened in a scuffle outside an off-licence between the licensee and the suspect. The licensee had refused to serve the suspect, who would not leave the premises. The suspect was warned by the police, but he continued to shout threats: "I'm going to get you, you bastard; that cunt did my friend... Why did you chuck me out, you fucking nigger?". He tried to push past the police back into the shop, waving his clenched fist at the manager. He was arrested.

HOME OFFICE RESEARCH STUDY No. 135

The question of why the police sometimes use section 5 in preference to other possible charges is discussed more fully elsewhere in this report. In the above example, it might be thought surprising that some form of assault charge was not brought, or a charge under sections 3 or 4 of the Public Order Act. However, the police may decide that section 5 is appropriate for several reasons: where, for example, there appears to be an element of fault on both sides and no clear victim or where the violence is minor. Section 5 may also be preferred where there are potential difficulties proving the case because the victim is unwilling to substantiate an allegation or it was not clear to police witnesses quite what happened.

'Indirect' victimisation

In just over a third of the cases in which the public were classed as victims (amounting to just over a quarter of all cases) there was no evidence of apparent distress on their part. Rather, the police simply referred to the likelihood of such distress. Sometimes this was made explicit by referring to the presence nearby of those the police regarded as vulnerable groups, particularly mothers and children or women generally. But reports were often less explicit, mentioning only that there were passers-by, without saying who they were or whether there was any discernible reaction to the offensive conduct.

The kinds of incident in which the public might be 'indirect' victims were those in which the culprits were acting in a violent or generally disorderly or rowdy manner, without apparently targeting their behaviour at uninvolved members of the public. The following is one of numerous examples:

> Durham, case 33: police officers observed the first suspect run shouting towards the second suspect and begin to fight with him. They were separated and warned about their conduct, but both continued to shout and swear. They were both arrested. The police report notes that 'several members of the public, including women, were in the vicinity at the time'.

One specific use of section 5 was to deal with public urination. This was treated as insulting behaviour which was likely to offend passers-by and as justifying a section 5 arrest.

In around a quarter of cases in which the public were 'indirect' victims, the primary target of the offensive conduct appeared to be the police. These cases are discussed more fully below. References in police reports to the presence of members of the public may have acted as a kind of insurance policy in case courts did not accept that police officers were harassed, alarmed or distressed.

The police as victims

In 28 per cent of cases (247 out of 881), police officers were the apparent victims of offensive conduct. In two-fifths (93) of these cases, the description of the incident does not suggest that there were any third parties present who were actually or likely to be offended and the police were therefore the sole victims. In the other three-fifths (154), members of the public were also present.

VICTIMS OF OFFENSIVE CONDUCT

The incidents ranged considerably in seriousness. In some cases, the facts as reported do not convey the impression that the conduct in question could be considered sufficient to harass, alarm or distress a police officer. In others, the events as described indeed sounded alarming. Whether or not violence was used is some guide to the level of seriousness (although it should be kept in mind that some assaults were technical ones only, while some instances of abuse or threats not culminating in violence could be extremely alarming). In all, nearly a quarter of cases in which the police were sole or joint victims were characterised by violence. In such cases, section 5 charges were often brought in conjunction with assault charges. The largest proportion of incidents - just under 60 per cent - were marked out by abusive or threatening behaviour towards the police.

Serious incidents

The following illustrate some of the kinds of cases which, from the accounts given, were situated at the more serious end of the spectrum. They show that the police at times have to endure considerable abuse and that genuine alarm or distress may be caused. In the first of these, the officer concerned was confronted with racial abuse, obscenities and threats of violence.

> Derby, case 14: the officer in the case saw two people alight from a taxi, having an argument, and he went up to them and asked if everything was alright. The suspect made a rude retort, and was warned by the PC. The suspect then allegedly countered: "What's it got to do with you, you wog? Do you cunts know who I am? I put two of you cunts in hospital; I'm (provides name)". He was warned again but replied: "I'll kick fuck out of you". He was then arrested.

In another case, police officers, one of whom was female, were subjected to insulting words and behaviour, and attempted violence.

> Vine Street, case 429: this incident arose from an earlier one, in which the suspect had accused the police of retaining a comb from his property after he had been detained at the police station. He returned to the police station early in the morning and began to be abusive to the officer at the counter. He was asked to leave. He started to hammer on a door to the station garage, told a female officer "fuck off, you bitch", and spat in her face. He then spat at another officer, continued to shout abuse and hurled a bread crate at a police officer. He was then arrested.

Less serious incidents

Incidents were generally not as serious as those described above. There were many in which it is doubtful whether the conduct concerned, as described in police reports, would genuinely have caused alarm or distress to a police officer. In the first example given below, the actions of the suspects may have struck no more than a blow to the officer's dignity.

> Durham, case 81: a van driven by the first suspect slowed down as it passed a police constable. The second suspect leaned out of the window and fired a water pistol at the PC, striking him in the face, and the vehicle then accelerated away.

In the second, the behaviour of the suspect was perhaps more irritating than alarming, but led to an arrest both under section 5 and for obstruction.

> Kirkby, case 75: a police officer was in the process of arresting another prisoner and gettng him into a police van when the suspect appeared and stood in the van doorway saying: "there's going to be fucking riots around here". He was told to go away, refused and was warned again. He then went round to the driver's door and slammed it in his face, 'alarming' him. He was subsequently arrested.

In the largest number of less serious cases the misconduct in question consisted of various abuse directed at the police. The language used generally amounted to fairly timeworn and familiar obscenities, which officers must have been well used to hearing. Whether they are likely to have been alarmed or distressed or felt that others nearby may have been is a matter for consideration. Two examples are given below.

> Hull, case 47: an officer stopped a car, in which the suspect - a known prostitute - was a passenger. The driver got out and accidentally fell as he did so. The suspect rounded on the officer and said: "you just fucking hit him". She was warned and replied: "you fucking shitheads, you just cost me forty fucking quid - you think you're something with that knob on your head". She was arrested.

> Vine Street, case 72: the suspect approached two officers and asked them if prostitution were illegal and, if so, why the police did nothing about it. "That fucking pimp round there's giving me hassle about a prostitute. But you won't fucking do nothing about it". The officers told him to calm down and they would sort the matter out. The suspect refused to calm down and replied: "I've already told you and you're not interested, fucking prancing around here doing nothing. You'll do nowt, you're a bunch of cunts". He was then arrested.

One group of cases is more problematic. Smith (1987) has suggested that, in the course of his duty, a police officer will become hardened to ritual taunts and insults. 'Ordinary' obscene language may be insufficient to cause the distress or alarm contemplated by section 5. Smith (ibid) notes that distress connotes some degree of perturbation and emotional upset, while alarm implies the experience of some fear or apprehension of danger. One ritual taunt, to which the police have become subject since the Broadwater Farm case, is the repetition of the word 'Blakelock'. While the circumstances of each case must be taken into account, it is debatable whether this taunt alone would usually be sufficient to cause the appropriate degree of distress to a police officer. However, in several cases in the sample it was taken as sufficient basis for making an arrest under section 5. In these circumstances, section 5 may have been used as a vehicle for asserting police authority where it was under threat rather than to cope with situations where officers were genuinely alarmed or distressed. The following is one example:

> Bristol Central, case 262: a police constable had attended an incident at a night-club. As he left, he heard one of a group of people outside repeating the word "Blakelock". The PC went up to the culprit and informed him that he found what he was saying intimidating and distressing, and that if he repeated it he would be arrested. The suspect followed the PC as he walked to his car and continued to shout "Blakelock" and "Thatcher's boot-boys". He was then arrested.

The presence of third parties

While the possibility that police officers may be harassed, alarmed or distressed has been recognised by the courts, police officers interviewed often pointed out that, in practice, it is not always easy to persuade magistrates of this. The necessity of doing so could be avoided simply by showing that there were other persons within sight or hearing who were likely to be caused harassment, alarm or distress by the behaviour in question. There is no requirement that such persons give evidence that they were alarmed; it is a matter for police judgement whether this likelihood existed.

This consideration may explain why a common feature of cases in which police officers were the targets of abuse was for arresting officers to make reference to the presence of passers-by. This protected officers against the possibility that magistrates would query whether the police themselves were offended. The facts of many cases suggest, however, that the primary purpose of arrest was to protect the police from abuse or threats or to reinforce respect. Thus, in nearly a quarter of the 247 cases in which the police were subjected to offensive conduct, there was little or no indication that passers-by were in any way offended but merely references to the presence of such persons. These references were often appended, as if as an after-thought, to offence reports. The following case illustrates these points:

> Hammersmith, case 231: two men were stopped in connection with a recent burglary. After some discussion one retorted: "no shit man, what are you trying to stitch me up with?" This suspect became increasingly aggressive and abusive while being questioned, shouting: "fuck off man, I've done nothing". He was warned about his behaviour by the police, whereupon he grabbed hold of one of the officer's arms and pushed him away, telling him: "fuck off man, just harass someone else". He was arrested. The report notes in conclusion that 'other persons were in the area at the time of the incident'.

In just over a third of the 247 cases, there were references to apparent distress on the part of members of the public. These lack force, however, because they were often tacked on to the end of police reports and provided little indication of the nature or extent of the distress. They often took the form of a brief statement that 'passers-by appeared distressed'. Given the circumstances of many incidents, it is questionable to what extent there may have been a real prospect of alarm or distress on the part of members of the public. Rowdy behaviour and taunts aimed at the police are routine features of Friday and

Saturday nights out in some city centres. Incidents often occurred when the streets were extremely noisy with people going home after a night out, and incidents may have gone largely unremarked or been accepted as 'normal'.

In some cases, however, it is clear that the public were affected by the incident as much as or more than the police, and police actions were not significantly motivated by the attitude towards them of the suspect. The following cases provide examples:

> Bristol City, case 1: the suspect was seen outside the police station in an agitated state, waving her fist in the air and shouting and swearing at passers-by. She crossed the road towards one woman, shouting "fucking come on then", and struggling with her before passers-by pulled her away. A police officer arrived on the scene and tried to calm her down. She rounded on him and told him to "fuck off". She repeated this and then punched him violently in the chest. She was then arrested.

> Kirkby, case 4: the suspect was at the centre of a large-scale disturbance involving about 20 people. He was accompanied by a large dog, which he was holding by the collar and pointing at the people, goading it with cries of "kill, kill". Several women and children were distinctly upset and crying. The suspect was shouting at one woman in particular "you're fucking dead". A police officer arrived and warned the suspect, who then tried to set the dog on the him. The officer had to use his truncheon to defend himself from the dog. The suspect was subsequently arrested.

Police tolerance of abuse

From many of the section 5 cases and from interviews with arresting officers, the impression comes across very strongly that what is at issue in many of the cases in which the police are the targets of abuse or threats is the enforcement of respect for the police. Arrest is a key resource for achieving this end and section 5 a convenient vehicle because it is very difficult for anyone later to query arresting officers' judgements about whether in the circumstances at the time they were harassed, alarmed or distressed. Since the decision in the Orum case, which effectively signalled to police officers that they may be harassed, alarmed or distressed, many have taken the view that they should no longer be expected to put up with the kind of abuse that, if directed at members of the public, would justify arrest. This is clearly reflected in the results of interviews with beat officers in the present study. Two-thirds stated that they would use section 5 to make an arrest in some circumstances in which they were the targets of abuse and where there were no bystanders. And, where there were bystanders but the police were nonetheless the main target, less than 10 per cent of officers reported that they would have any qualms about making an arrest.

Police officers may not in fact be greatly alarmed by abuse, but they are affected by it in other ways. They perceive that the public expects them to do something. They also perceive that if those who subject them to abuse realise that they can get away with it, respect for the police will decline further and they will be the targets of more abuse in future.

VICTIMS OF OFFENSIVE CONDUCT

Confronted by instances of abuse such as the following, police officers find it hard not to react:

> Derby, case 34: the suspect was one of two youths walking along a street shouting and swearing at the police. He was approached and warned and became more offensive, saying: "you bastard, if you didn't wear a fucking uniform I would kick fuck out of you and rip your head off".

> Kirkby, case 14: a police officer was in the process of making an arrest when he was approached by three persons behaving in a rowdy fashion. When they saw the PC one said: "let go of his arm you fucking queer". The PC warned him, but they carried on hurling abuse. For example: "he's only going to bum him - why don't you suck my cock you fucking big fat bastard?" The PC radioed for help and the youths were subsequently arrested.

In many section 5 cases in which the police are victims, the sequence of events is wearily familiar and predictable. The police receive abuse, either completely gratuitously, or during the course of making stops or arrests. They react by providing one or more warnings, as required by section 5 if an arrest is to be made, which further goads the suspect and leads to his or her arrest. In interviews, the police suggested that arrest was necessary in such situations in order to make a stand against a growing tide of disrespect for the police and to show suspects where the line should be drawn. It is hard to believe that, given the apparent attitudes to the police of those involved and the circumstances of the offences, arrest does in fact serve these ends. However, it is also difficult to argue with the police point of view that they should not be expected to withstand grossly insulting and obscene language. It is unlikely that many officers would accept that the best way to deal with situations in which they were abused would be to walk away from them.

HOME OFFICE RESEARCH STUDY No. 135

6 Proceedings and their outcome

Among the benefits of section 5 which the police commonly perceive is that it marks a case out as being more serious than, for example, an offence of drunk and disorderly. They maintain that it enables offenders to be put before the court rather than being dealt with by way of a caution or informal action. Arresting officers' views of the seriousness of cases may not always be reflected by those who have to review them. Mention has already been made, for example, of the fact that courts are not always comfortable with the notion that police officers may be alarmed or distressed by offensive conduct.

This chapter looks at the disposition of section 5 cases after arrest, up to and including sentence. Custody officers first take the decision whether to charge and, if so, with what offence. Secondly, before the case is submitted to the CPS it will be examined by police Administrative Support Units (or their equivalents). Thirdly, the case is reviewed by the CPS. They may decide to proceed on the charges as submitted, but they also have discretion to terminate proceedings if the evidence is insufficient or if they consider that it is not in the public interest to proceed, despite the sufficiency of the evidence. They may also vary the charges or accept an undertaking from the defendant to be bound over to keep the peace instead of proceeding. Lastly, where the case is heard, the court may dismiss the case or award a nominal penalty where they consider the proceedings unmeritorious.

The decision to proceed

Mode of proceeding

The great majority of proceedings in section 5 cases are by way of arrest and charge. Proceedings by way of summons are not precluded but they only accounted for 6 per cent of cases in which action was taken against a suspect. Under section 5(4), there is a specific power of arrest where a person engages in offensive conduct which a constable warns him to stop and where he then engages in further offensive conduct. In the typical situation in which section 5 is used, arrest is the most appropriate course. Suspects are often drunk and rowdy and order can only be restored by removing one or more of those involved. Nor are the parties generally in a reasonable enough frame of mind to make the taking of names and addresses for service of a summons practicable.

Summonsing may sometimes be appropriate where, for example, offensive behaviour is reported to an officer after the event and there is no opportunity to warn the offender to desist. However, the police may be reluctant to use the section in this kind of situation because it complicates the procedure and, in particular, requires witness statements to be taken rather than allowing the eye-witness evidence of police officers to suffice. At two stations - Kirkby and Grimsby - the proportions summonsed were far higher than average

(16 and 20 per cent respectively). At the former this was related to the fact that a far higher than average proportion of offenders were juveniles. Such cases are referred for consideration to the force's juvenile bureau, and this was treated in the research as equivalent to a report for summons. At the latter, most cases reported for summons involved public urination. In the absence of any aggravating factor it was not thought necessary to arrest (and suspects' capacity to continue the offending behaviour when warned to stop was inevitably finite!)

In over 90 per cent of cases in which some action was taken against the suspect this followed arrest. Indeed, where an arrest for a section 5 offence was made, it was unusual for action of some kind not to be taken. Only 4 per cent of those arrested were released without any further action, while just 1 per cent were bailed pending further enquiries. These proportions are far lower than for offences generally: Brown (1989) found that around 12 per cent of suspects are released without further action and another 12 per cent are bailed pending police enquiries. However, the high rate of proceeding is not surprising because difficulties about the sufficiency of evidence, which are at the root of decisions to release or bail for many other kinds of offence, are less likely to arise for section 5 offences. In order that the offence may be made out, it is enough that the arresting officer reasonably suspects that particular conduct is likely to cause harassment, alarm or distress. Custody officers are not well placed to question arresting officers' assessments after the event and, unless there are obvious omissions - for example, of the requirement to issue a warning - they will decide to set proceedings in motion.

Those arrested were generally charged. In only 7 per cent of cases in which some action was taken was the suspect cautioned. There are two reasons why this figure is so low. First, well over 90 per cent of suspects in the sample were aged over 16. Home Office Circular 59/90, which sought to extend cautioning to older age groups was only distributed in mid-1990. This was probably too late for any noticeable effect to have been felt prior to the end of that year. Second, some forces appear to have had a policy of charging in section 5 cases, although they would caution for other minor public order offences. The reason for this may have been to rank section 5 and drunk and disorderly cases in terms of seriousness and allow section 5 offenders to be dealt with by the court. This was not an invariable rule, although it was particularly noticeable in the Metropolitan Police, where around two-thirds of drunk and disorderly offenders were cautioned, compared with less than 10 per cent of section 5 suspects.

Discontinuance of proceedings by the CPS

Only 4 per cent of cases were discontinued by the Crown Prosecution Service,[1] with proceedings being terminated in 1 per cent of cases before they came to court, and in the other 3 per cent no evidence being offered at court. As outlined above, CPS decisions are arrived at following a review of the case. Proceedings may be discontinued if, in their view, there is insufficient evidence to afford a realistic prospect of conviction. Even if the evidence is sufficient, a prosecution may be discontinued if it is not in the public interest to pursue it.

---

[1] Nationally, proceedings begun by the police are terminated by the CPS in around 11 per cent of all cases.

PROCEEDINGS AND THEIR OUTCOME

The offence may be too trivial, for example, to merit prosecution. There was no evidence that the CPS were any more likely to discontinue cases in which police officers rather than members of the public were the victims of offensive behaviour. This might have been expected if the CPS had wished to mark section 5 out as aimed primarily at misconduct which alarms the public.

Court proceedings

Outcome

Two-thirds of defendants were found guilty, while nearly 10 per cent of cases were dismissed by the magistrates. The distinguishing feature of court proceedings in section 5 cases was the frequency with which defendants entered into recognizances to be of good behaviour (i.e. were bound over) without the case going to trial. Of nearly 900 defendants who appeared at court, 19 per cent agreed to a bind-over. This may represent a satisfactory resolution of relatively minor cases. It avoids the time and expense of court proceedings without suggesting - as discontinuance might - that police actions in putting the case forward for prosecution were necessarily unjustified. However, officers interviewed did not always see CPS decisions in this light. In their view, the CPS often tended to regard section 5 offences as relatively minor and not justifying the expense of proceedings. They felt that, had the defendant not agreed to a bind-over, the alternative would have been termination of proceedings. Nor was a bind-over necessarily seen as a satisfactory outcome by arresting officers. First, some cases were seen as too serious. Examples given in this report show that section 5 offences are not invariably trivial and may represent situations that are alarming for the public or the police. In some cases, the element of violence is such that the charges initially brought were under section 4 of the Public Order Act (fear or provocation of violence), only later being downgraded to section 5. Secondly, several officers considered that bind-overs were sometimes obtained without a proper evaluation of their appropriateness and, in particular, of the likelihood that the defendant would reoffend.

Sentence

Excluding those cases in which defendants were bound over, there were 620 members of the sample who were found guilty and sentenced. The usual penalty, awarded in three-quarters of cases, was a fine. Three per cent were placed on probation orders and 1 per cent were given community service orders. One-fifth of defendants received only a nominal penalty: most were given conditional discharges but 16 received an absolute discharge.

There were variations in the pattern of sentencing according to the type of case. It was far more common for those involved in incidents related to domestic disputes to be given a conditional discharge: over half of such cases that were heard by the courts were dealt with in this way. There were also differences in sentencing depending on whether police or public were the victims. Despite police contentions that courts sometimes appeared reluctant to accept that police officers could be victims in section 5 cases, there was a tendency for those who aimed abuse or threats at the police to be dealt with more severely. Three-quarters of this group received fines and less than 20 per cent conditional discharges, while of those whose misconduct was directed at members of the public, two-thirds were fined and nearly one-third given a conditional discharge. This suggests that police willingness to use section 5 in situations in which they are themselves the targets is an approach which is being backed up by the courts.

7 Conclusions

This report has examined the way in which section 5 of the Public Order Act is used in a range of police areas. It was found that the level of use varied considerably and that, while in some areas it was clear that section 5 was being employed in preference to other provisions that covered similar misconduct, elsewhere the new offence was not extensively used.

The most frequent use of section 5 was to deal with a broad spectrum of abusive or threatening behaviour in public places, although there was also some use to deal with violent or potentially violent situations. Section 5 was also sometimes called into play to deal with domestic disputes, indecency and football-related disorder. A large proportion of section 5 offences was concentrated into a relatively short period of time over the weekend, reflecting the fact that many incidents amounted to alcohol related disorder in and around entertainment centres.

There was some evidence that Afro-Caribbeans were over-represented among section 5 offenders in at least one police area (elsewhere, adequate data on ethnicity were not readily available). The kinds of incidents in which Afro-Caribbeans were involved also disproportionately involved abuse or threats directed at the police. The report suggests that one reason for this is that encounters between police and Afro-Caribbeans contain greater potential for friction and are more likely to degenerate into hostility and subsequent arrest under section 5.

An important finding was that, in a substantial minority of incidents, police officers were treated as the victims of offensive conduct - a situation that is not precluded by the legislation although it may not have been anticipated. It is for consideration whether the conduct used to justify arrest was always sufficient to alarm or distress police officers. Furthermore, in a third of cases in which members of the public were apparently viewed as victims, there were doubts about whether any real alarm was caused. Police actions in arresting for section 5 offences were not always backed up by action taken later by the Crown Prosecution Service or the courts. In around a fifth of cases forwarded to the CPS, the case did not go to a hearing and the offender agreed to a bind-over. A fifth of cases proceeding to a hearing ended with a nominal penalty for the defendant.

Is section 5 being used appropriately?

The extent to which section 5 is used in some areas and the circumstances in which arrests are made raise important questions about whether this provision of the Public Order Act is being used appropriately. Although there are minority uses of section 5 - for example, to deal with domestic arguments - very many incidents are characterised by abusive and disorderly behaviour, often drink-related, concentrated in and around city centre entertainment areas at the weekend.

Given the preparedness of the police to use arrest as a resource to restore public order, the outcome of many encounters between the participants and the police has a certain inevitability. The requirement for a section 5 arrest that at least one warning to desist from offensive conduct be given often appears to be a factor which is instrumental in provoking further disorderly behaviour and therefore justifying an arrest. The offending party or parties are typically in no reasonable frame of mind to respond to a warning. Police intervention is more than likely viewed as a challenge to which they need to respond with counter-challenge, whether to maintain their status in the eyes of their peers or simply to demonstrate their lack of respect for the police. This continuation or escalation of disorder when the police intervene is a persistent theme running through many section 5 cases.

The basis for police intervention in these situations is sometimes that the offensive behaviour is causing alarm and distress to others in the vicinity. However, reference to the presence of passers-by sometimes has the ring of being a technical device that can be used to justify arrest where the real issue is that of maintaining respect for the police. In an important minority of cases, no reference at all is made to the public as victims and it is clear that use of section 5 is justified largely on the grounds that the police are victims.

It is arguable whether in some section 5 cases any useful purpose is served by arresting. It is for consideration whether arrest is sometimes resorted to over-readily without exploring other options. This is not to deny that, in some cases, the police have little choice but to arrest: for example, where a fight is in progress and immediate action must be taken. More frequently, the situation has not reached this stage when the police intervene.

When arrest does eventually occur, following the typical spiral of warning/abuse/arrest, it is uncertain whether the reasoning the police use to justify their action can always be sustained. First, in the circumstances in which many incidents occur there are grounds for questioning whether members of the public in the vicinity are genuinely likely to be alarmed or distressed. City centre disorder when licensed premises close at the weekend is a commonplace for many of those who resort to these areas for entertainment. Secondly, while much of the bad language and abuse directed at the police themselves may be grossly insulting, it is doubtful whether it is generally such as would be likely to cause alarm or distress except to unduly sensitive officers. Most will have frequently heard the kind of taunts and language used. Thirdly, if the underlying reason for arresting is to instil respect for the police, it is very doubtful whether this object is achieved. The attitudes of the participants to the police are likely to be deeply grounded and not to be shaken by being arrested. They may indeed be reinforced by such adversarial encounters. Often those arrested are under the influence of alcohol. It is unlikely that arrest will have any effect on future behaviour when they are next under the uninhibiting effects of drink.

CONCLUSIONS

The most likely outcome if the case proceeds (a small fine, a bind-over or a nominal penalty) is likely to inconvenience the offender little.

The main purpose which arrest does serve in these situations is to restore order by removing the participants from the streets. If this is the primary - and achievable - aim, there seems little justification for using section 5 as the means of realising it, involving as it does the specific requirements of issuing warnings and showing that there were persons likely to be alarmed or distressed. It is probably for this reason that, in some areas, provisions other than section 5 were used, which are designed purely to remove the source of trouble. Hence, the predilection of the police for arresting for drunk and disorderly in Merseyside and for breach of the peace in Grimsby.

Whether section 5 or other provisions are used, police actions in low-level public order situations demonstrate their preference for arrest as the means to resolve the problem. The way that public order policing in some urban centres is organised also predisposes towards confrontation and arrest when trouble arises. Officers are frequently deployed in groups of six or more in incident vans with the primary aim of responding quickly to instances of disorder. Making arrests provides a tangible measure of the impact of this strategy. Also, because the response is in force, officers deployed in this way may feel less need to tread circumspectly or seek to resolve the situation short of arrest than officers who have in the first instance to deal with disorder on their own or with a single colleague. It is very easy in these circumstances for the situation to dissolve into the typical abuse/warning/arrest spiral.

It is for consideration whether there are other courses of action the police may take which could prevent incidents developing to a stage at which arrest is deemed necessary. There are several possibilities. One is for officers to exercise greater circumspection before making the initial intervention in a disorderly situation. Unless there is a real likelihood that a member of the public will suffer alarm or distress or is actually significantly affected by the offensive behaviour, the police may do well to let the situation ride for the time being. The mere presence of a police car or van may be sufficient in itself to have a deterrent effect. Early intervention, on the other hand may inflame matters. What it is reasonable to tolerate will depend on an appraisal of the situation in the light of the surrounding circumstances.

In some situations the police will have to intervene. However, despite the temptation to take action, they should be careful about doing so where they themselves are the targets of abuse because the dangers of escalation are greatest where there is overt hostility towards the police from the start. Furthermore, once locked into an encounter in which their objective is to deal with disrespect towards them, officers may have little option but to arrest in order to maintain face if the abusive behaviour continues. Such situations need to entered into with a realistic appraisal of the prospects of achieving any more positive result than the satisfaction of having retaliated against a challenge to police authority. It is unpalatable, but true, that the police will come in for considerable abuse in the course of their duties and that the wisest course may often be to ignore it.

HOME OFFICE RESEARCH STUDY No. 135

Once the decision is taken to intervene, it is for consideration whether there is scope for officers to be more flexible, both in their approach to dealing with disorder and in their attitudes to the potential outcome to the encounter. Rather than defining a situation as a prospective section 5 offence from the outset and therefore entering the spiral that begins with issuing a warning, officers may do well to approach low-level disorder with the view that the situation may be resolved by methods short of arrest. This may mean simply advising the party or parties to move on or seeking assistance from friends of the offender in getting them home where they are drunk and abusive.

It is not intended to suggest that section 5 should not be used where members of the public are genuinely likely to, or actually do, suffer significant harassment, alarm or distress as a result of offensive conduct. The opposite is in fact the case. If section 5 were reserved for precisely these situations, instead of being used as a broad spectrum offence to deal with what are basically 'drunk and disorderly' situations, it would become a more efficacious provision. By being identified primarily with relatively minor instances of disorder in which the police are abused and in which the public suffer little real detriment, it may fall into disrepute. One result may be that the courts may be unwilling to mark with appropriate severity those cases in which section 5 is used, as originally intended, to deal with behaviour that genuinely alarms members of the public. There is a corollary: that in areas where section 5 is little used to deal with behaviour that alarms members of the public, it should be used more. Other public order measures - particularly drunk and disorderly - should be confined to the behaviour for which they were intended.

There is a danger that section 5 may fall into disrepute if it is used disproportionately against members of ethnic minorities. There is some tentative evidence of such disproportionate use from the present study. One reason suggested for this over-representation is that encounters between Afro-Caribbeans and the police are more likely to engender friction. Firstly, hostility towards the police may be much nearer the surface in such encounters. And, secondly, the police may be more tense in dealing with such situations, particularly where a crowd rapidly gathers, as occurred in a number of examples given in Chapter 4. In these highly charged circumstances, there is the likelihood that the spiral of abuse/warning/arrest, that is a feature of section 5 cases, will be entered more readily. The solution to this problem is little different from the solution to dealing with problematic uses of section 5 generally. In other words, there is a need before issuing a section 5 warning for greater reflection about the possible consequences in terms of escalation of the situation, about the degree of alarm or distress genuinely caused to those in the vicinity or to the police themselves, and about the benefits that an arrest would actually achieve.

References

BIRCH, D. (1988). Case note on D.P.P. v. Orum. *Criminal Law Review*, 848-850.

FIELD, S. (1984). *The Attitudes of Ethnic Minorities*. Home Office Research Study No. 80. London: HMSO.

FIELD, S. (1990). *Trends in Crime and their Interpretation: a study of recorded crime in post-war England and Wales*. Home Office Research Study No. 119. London: HMSO.

HASKEY, J. (1991). 'The ethnic minority populations resident in private households - estimates by county and metropolitan district of England and Wales'. *Population Trends*, (63), 22-35.

HOME OFFICE. (1985). *Review of Public Order Law*. Cmnd. 9510. London: HMSO.

MCBARNET, D. (1981). *Conviction*. London: Macmillan.

NEWBURN, T., BROWN, D., CRISP, D. and DEWHURST, P. (1991). 'Increasing Public Order'. *Policing*, (7), 22-41.

NEWBURN, T., BROWN, D., CRISP, D. and DEWHURST, P. (1990). 'Policing the streets'. *Research Bulletin*, 10-14. Home Office Research and Statistics Department.

OFFICE OF POPULATION CENSUSES AND SURVEYS. (1992). *Labour Force Survey 1990-91*. London: HMSO.

OFFICE OF POPULATION CENSUSES AND SURVEYS (1993). 1991 Census: report for Great Britain (3 vols). London: HMSO.

OWEN, D. (1992). *Ethnic Minorities in Great Britain: settlement patterns*. University of Warwick Centre for Research in Ethnic Relations. National Ethnic Minority Data Archive: 1991 Census Statistical Paper No.1.

RAMSAY, M. (1982). *City Centre Crime: a situational approach to prevention*. Home Office Research and Planning Unit Paper 10. London: Home Office.

SKOGAN, W. (1990). *The Police and Public in England and Wales: a British Crime Survey Report*. Home Office Research Study No. 117. London: HMSO.

SMITH, D.J. (1983). *Police and People in London 1: a survey of Londoners*. London: Policy Studies Institute.

SMITH, A.T.H. (1987). *Offences against Public Order*. London: Sweet and Maxwell.

SOUTHGATE, P. and CRISP, D. (1993). *Public Satisfaction with Police Services*. Research and Planning Unit Paper 73. London: Home Office.

STEVENS, P. and WILLIS, C.F. (1979). *Race, Crime and Arrests*. Home Office Research Study No. 58. London: HMSO.

THORNTON, P. (1987). *Public Order Law*. London: Financial Training Publications Limited.

TUCK, M. (1989). *Drinking and Disorder: a study of non-metropolitan violence*. Home Office Research Study No. 108. London: HMSO.

WOOD, T. and GOODALL, K.E. (n.d.). *Serious Assault: an analysis and a strategy*. Report to Lothian and Borders Police. Unpublished.

Publications

The Research and Planning Unit (previously the Research Unit) has been publishing its work since 1955, and a full list of Papers is provided below. These reports are available on request from the Home Office Research and Planning Unit, Information Section, Room 278, 50 Queen Anne's Gate, London SW1H 9AT. Telephone: 071-273 2084 (answerphone).

Reports published in the HORS series are available from HMSO, who will advise as to prices, at the following address: :

HMSO Publications Centre
PO Box 276
London SW8 5DT

Telephone orders: 071-873 9090

General enquiries: 071-873 0011

Titles already published for the Home Office

Studies in the Causes of Delinquency and the Treatment of Offenders (SCDTO)

1. Prediction methods in relation to borstal training. Hermann Mannheim and Leslie T. Wilkins. 1955. viii + 276pp. (11 340051 9)

2. Time spent awaiting trial. Evelyn Gibson. 1960. v + 45pp. (34-368-2).

3. Delinquent generations. Leslie T. Wilkins. 1960. iv + 20pp. (11 340053 5).

4. Murder. Evelyn Gibson and S. Klein. 1961. iv + 44pp. (11 340054 3).

5. Persistent criminals. A study of all offenders liable to preventive detention in 1956. W.H. Hammond and Edna Chayen. 1963. ix + 237pp.(34-368-5).

6. Some statistical and other numerical techniques for classifying individuals. P.McNaughton-Smith. 1965. v + 33pp (34-368-6).

7. Probation research: a preliminary report. Part I. General outline of research. Part II. Study of Middlesex probation area (SOMPA) Steven Folkard, Kate Lyon, Margaret M. Carver and Erica O'Leary. 1966.vi + 58pp. (11 340374 7).

8. Probation research: national study of probation. Trends and regional comparisons in probation (England and Wales). Hugh Barr and Erica O'Leary. 1966. vii + 51pp. (34-368-8).

9. Probation research. A survey of group work in the probation service. Hugh Barr. 1966. vii + 94pp. (34-368-9).

10. Types of delinquency and home background. A validation study of Hewitt and Jenkins' hypothesis. Elizabeth Field. 1967. vi + 21pp. (34-368-10).

HOME OFFICE RESEARCH STUDY No.135

11. Studies of female offenders. No. 1 - Girls of 16-20 years sentenced to borstal or detention centre training in 1963. No. 2 - Women offenders in the Metropolitan Police District in March and April 1957. No. 3 - A description of women in prison on January 1, 1965. Nancy Goodman and Jean Price. 1967. v + 78pp. (34-368-11).

12. The use of the Jesness Inventory on a sample of British probationers. Martin Davies. 1967. iv + 20pp. (34-368-12).

13. The Jesness Inventory: application to approved school boys. Joy Mott. 1969. iv + 27pp. (11 340063 2).

Home Office Research Studies (HORS)

(Nos 1–106 are out of print)

1. Workloads in children's departments. Eleanor Grey. 1969. vi + 75pp. (11 340101 9).

2. Probationers in their social environment. A study of male probationers aged 17-20, together with an analysis of those reconvicted within twelve months. Martin Davies. 1969. vii + 204pp. (11 340102 7).

3. Murder 1957 to 1968. A Home Office Statistical Division report on murder in England and Wales. Evelyn Gibson and S. Klein (with annex by the Scottish Home and Health Department on murder in Scotland). 1969. vi + 94pp. (11 340103 5).

4. Firearms in crime. A Home Office Statistical Division report on indictable offences involving firearms in England and Wales. A. D. Weatherhead and B. M. Robinson. 1970. viii + 39pp. (11 340104 3).

5. Financial penalties and probation. Martin Davies. 1970. vii + 39pp. (11 340105 1).

6. Hostels for probationers. A study of the aims, working and variations in effectiveness of male probafion hostels with special reference to the influence of the environment on delinquency. Ian Sinclair. 1971.x + 200pp. (11 340106 X).

7. Prediction methods in criminology - including a prediction study of young men on probation. Frances H. Simon. 1971. xi + 234pp.(11 340107 8).

8. Study of the juvenile liaison scheme in West Ham 1961-65. Marilyn Taylor. 1971. vi + 46pp. (11 340108 6).

9. Explorations in after-care. I - After-care units in London, Liverpool and Manchester. Martin Silberman (Royal London Prisoners' Aid Society) and Brenda Chapman. II - After-care hostels receiving a Home Office grant. Ian Sinclair and David Snow (HORU). III - St. Martin of Tours House, Aryeh Leissner (National Bureau for Co-operation in Child Care). 1971. xi + 140pp. (11 340109 4).

10. A survey of adoption in Great Britain. Eleanor Grey in collaboration with Ronald M. Blunden. 1971. ix + 168pp. (11 340110 8).

11. Thirteen-year-old approved school boys in 1960s. Elizabeth Field, W H Hammond and J. Tizard. 1971.ix + 46pp. (11 340111 6).

12. Absconding from approved schools. R. V. G. Clarke and D. N. Martin. 1971. vi + 146pp.(11 340112 4).

13. An experiment in personality assessment of young men remanded in custody.
H. Sylvia Anthony. 1972. viii + 79pp. (11 340113 2).

14. Girl offenders aged 17-20 years. I - Statistics relating to girl offenders aged 17-20 years from 1960 to 1970. II - Re-offending by girls released from borstal or detention centre training. III - The problems of girls released from borstal training during their period on after-care. Jean Davies and Nancy Goodman.
1972. v + 77pp. (11 340114 0).

15. The controlled trial in institutional research - paradigm or pitfall for penal evaluators? R. V. G. Clarke and D. B. Cornish. 1972. v + 33pp. (11 340115 9).

16. A survey of fine enforcement. Paul Softley. 1973. v + 65pp. (11 340116 7).

17. An index of social environment - designed for use in social work research.
Martin Davies. 1973. vi + 63pp. (11 340117 5).

18. Social enquiry reports and the probation service. Martin Davies and Andrea Knopf.
1973. v + 49pp.(11 340118 3).

19. Depression, psychopathic personality and attempted suicide in a borstal sample.
H. Sylvia Anthony.1973. viii + 44pp. (0 11 340119 1).

20. The use of bail and custody by London magistrates' courts before and after the Criminal Justice Act 1967. Frances Simon and Mollie Weatheritt. 1974. vi + 78pp.
(0 11 340120 5).

21. Social work in the environment. A study of one aspect of probation practice.
Martin Davies, with Margaret Rayfield, Alaster Calder and Tony Fowles. 1974.
ix + 151pp. (0 11 340121 3).

22. Social work in prison. An experiment in the use of extended contact with offenders. Margaret Shaw.1974. viii + 154pp. (0 11 340122 1).

23. Delinquency amongst opiate users. Joy Mott and Marilyn Taylor. 1974.vi + 31pp.
(0 11 340663 0).

24. IMPACT. Intensive matched probation and after-care treatment. Vol. I - The design of the probation experiment and an interim evaluation. M. S. Folkard,
A. J. Fowles, B.C. McWilliams, W. McWilliams, D. D. Smith, D. E. Smith and
G. R. Walmsley. 1974. v + 54pp. (0 11 340664 9).

25. The approved school experience. An account of boys' experiences of training under differing regimes of approved schools,with an attempt to evaluate the effectiveness of that training. Anne B. Dunlop. 1974. vii + 124pp. (0 11 340665 7).

26. Absconding from open prisons. Charlotte Banks, Patricia Mayhew and
R. J. Sapsford. 1975. viii + 89pp. (0 11 340666 5).

27. Driving while disqualified. Sue Kriefman. 1975. vi + 136pp.(0 11 340667 3).

28. Some male offenders' problems. - Homeless offenders in Liverpool.
W. McWilliams. II - Casework with short-term prisoners. Julie Holborn. 1975.
x + 147pp. (0 11 340668 1).

HOME OFFICE RESEARCH STUDY No.135

29. Community service orders. K. Pease, P. Durkin, I. Earnshaw, D. Payne and J. Thorpe. 1975. viii + 80pp.(0 11 340669 X).

30. Field Wing Bail Hostel: the first nine months. Frances Simon and Sheena Wilson. 1975. viii + 55pp. (0 11 340670 3).

31. Homicide in England and Wales 1967-1971. Evelyn Gibson. 1975. iv + 59pp. (0 11 340753 X).

32. Residential treatment and its effects on delinquency. D. B. Cornish and R. V. G. Clarke. 1975. vi + 74pp. (0 11 340672 X).

33. Further studies of female offenders. Part A: Borstal girls eight years after release. Nancy Goodman, Elizabeth Maloney and Jean Davies. Part B: The sentencing of women at the London Higher Courts. Nancy Goodman, Paul Durkin and Janet Halton. Part C: Girls appearing before a juvenile court. Jean Davies. 1976. vi + 114pp. (0 11 340673 8).

34. Crime as opportunity. P. Mayhew, R. V. G. Clarke, A. Sturman and J. M. Hough. 1976. vii + 36pp.(0 11 340674 6).

35. The effectiveness of sentencing: a review of the literature. S. R. Brody. 1976. v + 89pp.(0 11 340675 4).

36. IMPACT. Intensive matched probation and after-care treatment. Vol. II - The results of the experiment. M. S. Folkard, D. E. Smith and D. D. 1976. xi + 40pp. (0 11 340676 2).

37. Police cautioning in England and Wales. J. A. Ditchfield. 1976. v + 31pp. (0 11 340677 0).

38. Parole in England and Wales. C. P. Nuttall, with E. E. Barnard, A. J. Fowles, A. Frost, W. H. Hammond, P. Mayhew, K. Pease, R. Tarling and M. J. Weatheritt. 1977. vi + 90pp. (0 11 340678 9).

39. Community service assessed in 1976. K. Pease, S. Billingham and I. Earnshaw. 1977. vi + 29pp.(0 11 340679 7).

40. Screen violence and film censorship: a review of research. Stephen Brody. 1977. vii + 179pp.(0 11 340680 0).

41. Absconding from borstals. Gloria K. Laycock. 1977. v + 82pp. (0 11 340681 9).

42. Gambling: a review of the literature and its implications for policy and research. D. B. Cornish. 1978.xii + 284pp. (0 11 340682 7).

43. Compensation orders in magistrates' courts. Paul Softley. 1978. v + 41pp. (0 11 340683 5).

44. Research in criminal justice. John Croft. 1978. iv + 16pp. (0 11 340684 3).

45. Prison welfare: an account of an experiment at Liverpool. A. J. Fowles. 1978. v + 34pp. (0 11 340685 1).

46. Fines in magistrates' courts. Paul Softley. 1978. v + 42pp. (0 11 340686 X).

47. Tackling vandalism. R. V. Clarke (editor), F. J. Gladstone, A. Sturman and Sheena Wilson 1978. vi + 91pp. (0 11 340687 8).

48. Social inquiry reports: a survey. Jennifer Thorpe. 1979. vi + 55pp. (0 11 340688 6).

49. Crime in public view. P. Mayhew, R. V. G. Clarke, J. N. Burrows, J. M. Hough and S. W. C. Winchester. 1979. v + 36pp. (0 11 340689 4).

50. Crime and the community. John Croft. 1979. v + 16pp. (0 11 340690 8).

51. Life-sentence prisoners. David Smith (editor), Christopher Brown, Joan Worth, Roger Sapsford and Charlotte Banks (contributors). 1979. iv + 51pp. (0 11 340691 6).

52. Hostels for offenders. Jane E. Andrews, with an appendix by Bill Sheppard. 1979. v + 30pp. (0 11 340692 4).

53. Previous convictions, sentence and reconviction: a statistical study of a sample of 5,000 offenders convicted in January 1971. G. J. O. Phillpotts and L. B. Lancucki. 1979. v + 55pp. (0 11 340693 2).

54. Sexual offences, consent and sentencing. Roy Walmsley and Karen White. 1979. vi + 77pp.(0 11 340694 0).

55. Crime prevention and the police. John Burrows, Paul Ekblom and Kevin Heal. 1979. v + 37pp. (0 11 340695 9).

56. Sentencing practice in magistrates' courts. Roger Tarling, with the assistance of Mollie Weatheritt. 1979. vii + 54pp. (0 11 340696 7).

57. Crime and comparative research. John Croft. 1979. iv + 16pp. (0 11 340697 5).

58. Race, crime and arrests. Philip Stevens and Carole F. Willis. 1979. v + 69pp. (0 11 340698 3).

59. Research and criminal policy. John Croft. 1980. iv + 14pp. (0 11 340699 1).

60. Junior attendance centres. Anne B. Dunlop. 1980. v + 47pp. (0 11 340700 9).

61. Police interrogation: an observational study in four police stations. Paul Softley, with the assistance of David Brown, Bob Forde, George Mair and David Moxon. 1980. vii + 67pp. (0 11 340701 7).

62. Co-ordinating crime prevention efforts. F. J. Gladstone. 1980. v + 74pp. (0 11 340702 5).

63. Crime prevention publicity: an assessment. D. Riley and P. Mayhew. 1980. v + 47pp.(0 11 340703 3).

64. Taking offenders out of circulation. Stephen Brody and Roger Tarling. 1980. v + 46pp.(0 11 340704 1).

65. Alcoholism and social policy: are we on the right lines? Mary Tuck. 1980. v + 30pp. (0 11 340705 X).

66. Persistent petty offenders. Suzan Fairhead. 1981. vi + 78pp. (0 11 340706 8).

HOME OFFICE RESEARCH STUDY No.135

67. Crime control and the police. Pauline Morris and Kevin Heal. 1981. v + 71pp. (0 11 340707 6).

68. Ethnic minorities in Britain: a study of trends in their position since 1961. Simon Field, George Mair, Tom Rees and Philip Stevens. 1981. v + 48pp. (0 11 340708 4).

69. Managing criminological research. John Croft. 1981. iv + 17pp. (0 11 340709 2).

70. Ethnic minorities, crime and policing: a survey of the experiences of West Indians and whites. Mary Tuck and Peter Southgate. 1981. iv + 54pp. (0 11 340765 3).

71. Contested trials in magistrates' courts. Julie Vennard. 1982. v + 32pp. (0 11 340766 1).

72 Public disorder: a review of research and a study in one inner city area. Simon Field and Peter Southgate. 1982. v + 77pp. (0 11 340767 X).

73. Clearing up crime. John Burrows and Roger Tarling. 1982. vii + 31pp. (0 11 340768 8).

74. Residential burglary: the limits of prevention. Stuart Winchester and Hilary Jackson. 1982. v + 47pp. (0 11 340769 6).

75. Concerning crime. John Croft. 1982. iv + 16pp. (0 11 340770 X).

76. The British Crime Survey: first report. Mike Hough and Pat Mayhew. 1983. v + 62pp. (0 11 340786 6).

77. Contacts between police and public: findings from the British Crime Survey. Peter Southgate and Paul Ekblom. 1984. v + 42pp. (0 11 340771 8).

78. Fear of crime in England and Wales. Michael Maxfield. 1984. v + 57pp. (0 11 340772 6).

79. Crime and police effectiveness. Ronald V Clarke and Mike Hough 1984. iv + 33pp. (0 11 340773 3).

80. The attitudes of ethnic minorities. Simon Field. 1984. v + 49pp. (0 11 340774 2).

81. Victims of crime: the dimensions of risk. Michael Gottfredson. 1984. v + 54pp. (0 11 340775 0).

82. The tape recording of police interviews with suspects: an interim report. Carole Willis.1984.v + 45pp.(0 11 340776 9).

83. Parental supervision and juvenile delinquency. David Riley and Margaret Shaw. 1985.v + 90pp.(0 11 340799 8).

84. Adult prisons and prisoners in England and Wales 1970-1982: a review of the findings of social research. Joy Mott. 1985. vi + 73pp. (0 11 340801 3).

85. Taking account of crime: key findings from the 1984 British Crime Survey. Mike Hough and Pat Mayhew. 1985. vi + 115pp. (0 11 341810 2).

86. Implementing crime prevention measures. Tim Hope. 1985. vi + 82pp. (0 11 340812 9).

87. Resettling refugees: the lessons of research. Simon Field. 1985. vi + 66pp. (0 11 340815 3).

88. Investigating burglary: the measurement of police performance. John Burrows. 1986. vi + 36pp.(0 11 340824 2)

89. Personal violence. Roy Walmsley. 1986. vi + 87pp. (0 11 340827 7).

90. Police-public encounters. Peter Southgate. 1986. vi + 150pp. (0 11 340834 X).

91. Grievance procedures in prisons. John Ditchfield and Claire Austin. 1986. vi + 87pp. (0 11 340839 0).

92. The effectiveness of the Forensic Science Service. Malcolm Ramsay. 1987. v + 100pp.(0 11 340842 0).

93. The police complaints procedure: a survey of complainant's views. David Brown. 1987. v + 98pp. (0 11 340853 6).

94. The validity of the reconviction prediction score. Denis Ward. 1987. vi + 46. (0 11 340882 X).

95. Economic aspects of the illicit drug market enforcement policies in the United Kingdom. Adam Wagstaff and Alan Maynard. 1988. vii + 156pp. (0 11 340883 8)

96. Schools, disruptive behaviour and deliquency: a review of literature. John Graham. 1988. v + 70pp. (0 11 340887 0).

97. The tape recording of police interviews with suspects: a second interim report. Carole Willis, John Macleod and Peter Naish. 1988. vii + 97pp. (011 340890 0).

98. Triable-either-way cases: Crown Court or magistrate's court. David Riley and Julie Vennard. 1988. v + 52pp. (0 11 340891 9).

99. Directing patrol work: a study of uniformed policing. John Burrows and Helen Lewis. 1988 v + 66pp. (0 11 340891 9)

100. Probation day centres. George Mair. 1988. v + 44pp. (0 11 340894 3).

101. Amusement machines: dependency and delinquency. John Graham. 1988. v + 48pp. (0 11 340895 1).

102. The use and enforcement of compensation orders in magistrates' courts. Tim Newburn. 1988. v + 49pp. (0 11 340 896 X)

103. Sentencing practice in the Crown Court. David Moxon. 1988. v + 90pp. (0 11 340902 8).

104. Detention at the police station under the Police and Criminal Evidence Act 1984. David Brown. 1988. v + 88pp. (0 113340908 7).

105. Changes in rape offences and sentencing. Charles Lloyd and Roy Walmsley. 1989. vi + 53pp.(0 11 340910 9).

106. Concerns about rape. Lorna Smith. 1989. v + 48pp. (0 11 340911 7).

107. Domestic violence. Lorna Smith. 1989. v + 132pp. (0 11 340925 7)

HOME OFFICE RESEARCH STUDY No.135

108. Drinking and disorder: a study of non-metropolitan violence. Mary Tuck. 1989. v + 111pp. (011 340926 5).

109. Special security units. Roy Walmsley. 1989. v + 114pp. (0 11 340961 3).

110. Pre-trial delay: the implications of time limits. Patricia Morgan and Julie Vennard. 1989. v + 66pp. (0 11 340964 8)

111. The 1988 British Crime Survey. Pat Mayhew, David Elliott and Lizanne Dowds. 1989. v + 133pp. (0 11 340965 6).

112. The settlement of claims at the Criminal Injuries Compensation Board. Tim Newburn. 1989. v + 40pp. (0 11 340967 2)

113. Race, community groups and service delivery. Hilary Jackson and Simon Field. 1989. v + 62pp.(0 11 340972 9)

114. Money payment supervision orders: probation policy and practice. George Mair and Charles Lloyd. 1989.v + 40pp. (0 11 340971 0).

115. Suicide and self-injury in prison: a literature review. Charles Lloyd. 1990. v + 69pp. (0 11 3409745 5).

116. Keeping in Touch: police-victim communication in two areas. Tim Newburn and Susan Merry. 1990. v + 52pp. (0 11 340974 5).

117. The police and public in England and Wales: a British Crime Survey report. Wesley G. Skogan. 1990. vi + 74pp. (0 11 340995 8).

118. Control in prisons: a review of the literature. John Ditchfield. 1990 (0 11 340996 6).

119. Trends in crime and their interpretation: a study of recorded crime in post-war England and Wales. Simon Field. 1990. (0 11 340994 X).

120. Electronic monitoring: the trials and their results. George Mair and Claire Nee. 1990. v + 79pp (0 11 340998 2).

121. Drink driving: the effects of enforcement. David Riley. 1991. viii + 78pp (0 11 340999 0).

122. Managing difficult prisoners: the Parkhurst Special Unit. Roy Walmsley (Ed.) 1991. x + 139pp (0 11 341008 5).

123. Investigating burglary: the effects of PACE. David Brown. 1991. xii + 106pp. (0 11 341011 5).

124. Traffic policing in changing times. Peter Southgate and Catriona Mirrlees-Black. 1991. viii + 139pp (0 11 341019 0)

125. Magistrates' court or Crown Court ? Mode of trial decisions and sentencing. Carol Hedderman and David Moxon. 1992. vii + 53pp. (0 11 341036 0).

126. Developments in the use of compensation orders in magistrates' courts since October 1988. David Moxon, John Martin Corkery and Carol Hedderman. 1992. x + 48pp. (0 11 341042 5).

127. A comparative study of firefighting arrangements in Britain, Denmark, the Netherlands and Sweden. John Graham, Simon Field, Roger Tarling and Heather Wilkinson. 1992. x + 57pp. (0 11 341043 3).

128. The National Prison Survey 1991: main findings. Roy Walmsley, Liz Howard and Sheila White. 1992. xiv + 82pp. (0 11 341051 4).

129. Changing the Code: police detention under the revised PACE Codes of Practice. David Brown, Tom Ellis and Karen Larcombe. 1992. viii + 122pp. (0 11 341052 2).

130. Car theft: the offender's perspective. Roy Light, Claire Nee and Helen Ingham. 1993. x + 89pp. (0 11 341069 7).

131. Housing, Community and Crime: The Impact of the Priority Estates Project. Janet Foster and Timothy Hope with assistance from Lizanne Dowds and Mike Sutton. 1993. xi + 118. (0 11 341078 6).

132. The 1992 British Crime Survey. Pat Mayhew, Natalie Aye Maung and Catriona Mirrlees-Black. 1993. xiii + 206. (0 11 341094 8).

Research and Planning Unit Papers (RPUP)

1. Uniformed police work and management technology. J. M. Hough. 1980.

2. Supplementary information on sexual offences and sentencing. Roy Walmsley and Karen White. 1980.

3. Board of visitor adjudications. David Smith, Claire Austin and John Ditchfield. 1981.

4. Day centres and probation. Suzan Fairhead, with the assistance of J.Wilkinson-Grey. 1981.

5. Ethnic minorities and complaints against the police. Philip Stevens and Carole Willis. 1982.

6. Crime and public housing. Mike Hough and Pat Mayhew (editors). 1982.

7. Abstracts of race relations research. George Mair and Philip Stevens (editors). 1982.

8. Police probationer training in race relations. Peter Southgate. 1982.

9. The police response to calls from the public. Paul Ekblom and Kevin Heal. 1982.

10. City centre crime: a situational approach to prevention. Malcolm Ramsay. 1982.

11. Burglary in schools: the prospects for prevention. Tim Hope. 1982.

12. Fine enforcement. Paul Softley and David Moxon. 1982.

13. Vietnamese refugees. Peter Jones. 1982.

14. Community resources for victims of crime. Karen Williams. 1983.

15. The use, effectiveness and impact of police stop and search powers. Carole Willis. 1983.

16. Acquittal rates. Sid Butler. 1983.

17. Criminal justice comparisons: the case of Scotland and England and Wales. Lorna J. F. Smith. 1983.

18. Time taken to deal with juveniles under criminal proceedings. Catherine Frankenburg and Roger Tarling. 1983.

HOME OFFICE RESEARCH STUDY No.135

19. Civilian review of complaints against the police: a survey of the United States literature. David C. Brown. 1983.
20. Police action on motoring offences. David Riley. 1983.
21. Diverting drunks from the criminal justice system. Sue Kingsley and George Mair. 1983.
22. The staff resource implications of an independent prosecution system. Peter R. Jones. 1983.
23. Reducing the prison population: an exploratory study in Hampshire. David Smith, Bill Sheppard, George Mair, Karen Williams. 1984.
24. Criminal justice system model: magistrates' courts sub-model. Susan Rice. 1984.
25. Measures of police effectiveness and efficiency. Ian Sinclair and Clive Miller. 1984.
26. Punishment practice by prison Boards of Visitors. Susan Iles, Adrienne Connors, Chris May, Joy Mott. 1984.
27. Reparation, conciliation and mediation: current projects and plans in England and Wales. Tony Marshall. 1984.
28. Magistrates' domestic courts: new perspectives. Tony Marshall (editor). 1984.
29. Racism awareness training for the police. Peter Southgate. 1984.
30. Community constables: a study of a policing initiative. David Brown and Susan Iles. 1985.
31. Recruiting volunteers. Hilary Jackson. 1985.
32. Juvenile sentencing: is there a tariff? David Moxon, Peter Jones, Roger Tarling. 1985.
33. Bringing people together: mediation and reparation projects in Great Britain. Tony Marshall and Martin Walpole. 1985.
34. Remands in the absence of the accused. Chris May. 1985.
35. Modelling the criminal justice system. Patricia M Morgan. 1985.
36. The criminal justice system model: the flow model. Hugh Pullinger. 1986.
37. Burglary: police actions and victim views. John Burrows. 1986.
38. Unlocking community resources: four experimental government small grants schemes. Hilary Jackson. 1986.
39. The cost of discriminating: a review of the literature. Shirley Dex. 1986.
40. Waiting for Crown Court trial: the remand population. Rachel Pearce. 1987.
41. Children's evidence: the need for corroboration. Carol Hedderman. 1987.
42. A prelimary study of victim offender mediation and reparation schemes in England and Wales. Gwynn Davis, Jacky Boucherat, David Watson, Adrian Thatcher (Consultant). 1987.

43. Explaining fear of crime: evidence from the 1984 British Crime Survey. Michael Maxfield. 1987.
44. Judgements of crime seriousness: evidence from the 1984 British Crime Survey. Ken Pease. 1988.
45. Waiting time on the day in magistrates' courts: a review of case listings practises. David Moxon and Roger Tarling (editors). 1988.
46. Bail and probation work: the ILPS temporary bail action project. George Mair. 1988.
47. Police work and manpower allocation. Roger Tarling. 1988.
48. Computers in the courtroom. Carol Hedderman. 1988.
49. Data interchange between magistrates' courts and other agencies. Carol Hedderman. 1988.
50. Bail and probation work II: the use of London probation/bail hostels for bailees. Helen Lewis and George Mair. 1989.
51. The role and function of police community liaison officers. Susan V Phillips and Raymond Cochrane. 1989.
52. Insuring against burglary losses. Helen Lewis. 1989.
53. Remand decisions in Brighton and Bournemouth. Patricia Morgan and Rachel Pearce. 1989.
54. Racially motivated incidents reported to the police. Jayne Seagrave. 1989.
55. Review of research on re-offending of mentally disordered offenders. David J. Murray. 1990.
56. Risk prediction and probation: papers from a Research and Planning Unit workshop. George Mair (editor). 1990.
57. Household fires: findings from the British Crime Survey 1988. Chris May. 1990.
58. Home Office funding of victim support schemes - money well spent? Justin Russell. 1990.
59. Unit fines: experiments in four courts. David Moxon, Mike Sutton and Carol Hedderman. 1990.
60. Deductions from benefit for fine default. David Moxon, Carol Hedderman and Mike Sutton. 1990.
61. Monitoring time limits on custodial remands. Paul F. Henderson. 1991.
62. Remands in custody for up to 28 days: the experiments. Paul F. Henderson and Patricia Morgan. 1991.
63. Parenthood training for young offenders: an evaluation of courses in Young Offender Institutions. Diane Caddle. 1991.
64. The multi-agency approach in practice: the North Plaistow racial harassment project. William Saulsbury and Benjamin Bowling. 1991.

HOME OFFICE RESEARCH STUDY No.135

65. Offending while on bail: a survey of recent studies. Patricia M. Morgan. 1992.
66. Juveniles sentenced for serious offences: a comparison of regimes in Young Offender Institutions and Local Authority Community Homes. John Ditchfield and Liza Catan. 1992.
67. The management and deployment of police armed response vehicles. Peter Southgate. 1992.
68. Using psychometric personality tests in the selection of firearms officers. Catriona Mirrlees-Black. 1992.
69. Bail information schemes: practice and effect. Charles Lloyd. 1992.
70. Crack and cocaine in England and Wales. Joy Mott (editor). 1992
71. Rape: from recording to conviction. Sharon Grace, Charles Lloyd and Lorna J.F. Smith. 1992.
72. The National Probation Survey 1990. Chris May. 1993.
73. Public satisfaction with police services. Peter Southgate and Debbie Crisp. 1993.
74. Disqualification from driving: an effective penalty?. Catriona Mirrlees-Black. 1993.
75. Detention under the Prevention of Terrorism (Temporary Provisions) Act 1989: Access to legal advice and outside contact. David Brown. 1993.
76. Panel assessment schemes for mentally disordered offenders. Carol Hedderman. 1993.
77. Cash-limiting the probation service: a case study in resource allocation. Simon Field and Mike Hough. 1993.
78. The probation response to drug misuse. Claire Nee and Rae Sibbitt. 1993.
79. Approval of rifle and target shooting clubs: the effects of the new and revised criteria. John Martin Corkery. 1993.
80. The long-term needs of victims: A review of the literature. Tim Newburn. 1993.
81. The welfare needs of unconvicted prisoners. Diane Caddle and Sheila White. 1994.
82. Racially motivated crime: a British Crime Survey analysis. Natalie Aye Maung and Catriona Mirrlees-Black. 1994.
83. Mathematical models for forecasting Passport demand. Andy Jones and John MacLeod. 1994.
84. Not published yet.
85. Equal opportunities and the Fire Service. Tom Bucke. 1994.

Research Findings

(These are summaries of reports and are also available from the Information Section)

1. Magistrates' court or Crown Court? Mode of trial decisions and their impact on sentencing. Carol Hedderman and David Moxon. 1992.
2. Surveying crime: findings from the 1992 British Crime Survey. Pat Mayhew and Natalie Aye Maung. 1992.
3. Car Theft: the offenders's perspective: Claire Nee. 1993.
4. The National Prison survey 1991: main findings. Roy Walmsley, Liz Howard and Sheila White. 1993.
5. Changing the Code: Police detention under the revised PACE codes of practice. David Brown, Tom Ellis and Karen Larcombe. 1993.
6. Rifle and pistol target shooting clubs: The effects of new approval criteria. John M Corkery. 1993.
7. Self-reported drug misuse in England and Wales. Main findings from the 1992 British Crime Survey. Joy Mott and Catriona Mirrlees-Black. 1993.
8. Findings from the International Crime Survey. Pat Mayhew. 1994.
9. Fear of Crime: Findings from the 1992 British Crime Survey. Catriona Mirrlees-Black and Natalie Aye Maung. 1994.
10. Does the Criminal Justice system treat men and women differently? Carol Hedderman and Mike Hough. 1994.
11. Participation in Neighbourhood Watch: Findings from the 1992 British Crime Survey. Lizanne Dowds and Pat Mayhew. 1994.

Research Bulletin (available from the Information Section)

The Research Bulletin is published twice a year and consists mainly of short articles relating to projects which are part of the Home Office Research and Planning Unit's research programme.

HOME OFFICE RESEARCH STUDY No.135

Occasional Papers

(These can be purchased from the main Home Office Library Publications Unit, 50 Queen Anne's Gate, London SWIH 9AT. Telephone 071-273 2302 for information on price and availability. Those marked with an asterisk are out of print.)

*The 'watchdog' role of Boards of Visitors. Mike Maguire and Jon Vagg. 1984.

Shared working between Prison and Probation Officers. Norman Jepson and Kenneth Elliot. 1985.

After-care Services for Released Prisoners: A Review of the Literature. Kevin Haines. 1990.

*Arts in Prisons: towards a sense of achievement. Anne Peaker and Jill Vincent. 1990.

Pornography: impacts and influences. Dennis Howitt and Guy Cumberbatch. 1990.

*An evaluation of the live link for child witnesses. Graham Davies and Elizabeth Noon. 1991.

Mentally disordered prisoners. John Gunn, Tony Maden and Mark Swinton. 1991.

Coping with a crisis: the introduction of three and two in a cell. T G Weiler. 1992.

Psychiatric Assessment at the Magistrates' Court. Philip Joseph. 1992.

Measurement of caseload weightings in magistrates' courts. Richard J Gadsden and Graham J Worsdale. 1992.

The CDE of scheduling in magistrates' courts. John W Raine and Michael J Willson. 1992.

Employment opportunities for offenders. David Downes. 1993.

Sex offenders: a framework for the evaluation of community-based treatment. Mary Barker and Rod Morgan. 1993.

Suicide attempts and self-injury in male prisons. Alison Liebling and Helen Krarup. 1993.

Measurement of caseload weightings associated with the Children's Act. Richard J Gadsden and Graham J Worsdale. 1994 (available from the RPU Information Section).

Managing difficult prisoners: The Lincoln and Hull special units.
Professor Keith Bottomley, Professor Norman Jepson, Mr Kenneth Elliott and Dr Jeremy Coid. 1994 (available from RPU Information Section).

The NACRO diversion initiative for mentally disturbed offenders: an account and an evaluation. Home Office - NACRO - Mental Health Foundation. 1994 (available from the RPU Information Section).

Other Publications by members of RPU (available from HMSO)

Designing out crime. R. V. G. Clarke and P. Mayhew (editors). 1980. viii + 186pp. (0 11 340732 7).

Policing today. Kevin Heal, Roger Tarling and John Burrows (editors). v + 181pp. (0 11 340800 5).

Managing criminal justice: a collection of papers. David Moxon (editor). 1985. vi + 222pp. (0 11 340811 0).

Situational crime prevention: from theory into practice. Kevin Heal and Gloria Laycock (editors). 1986. vii + 166pp. (0 11 340826 9)

Communities and crime reduction. Tim Hope and Margaret Shaw (editors). 1988. vii + 311pp. (11 340892 7).

New directions in police training. Peter Southgate (editor). 1988. xi + 256pp (11 340889 7).

Crime and Accountability: Victim/Offender Mediation in Practice. Tony F Marshall and Susan Merry. 1990. xii + 262. (0 11 340973 7).

Community Work and the Probation Service. Paul Henderson and Sarah del Tufo. 1991. vi + 120. (0 11 341004 2).

Part Time Punishment? George Mair. 1991. 258 pp. (0 11 340981 8).

Analysing Offending. Data, Models and Interpretations. Roger Tarling. 1993. viii + 203. (0 11 341080 8).